ATTACHED

Sarah,

ATTACHED

Thank you for your support. I hope you enjoy Ellie's story!

[signature]

Terece Hahn Metzger

NEW DEGREE PRESS
COPYRIGHT © 2022 TERECE HAHN METZGER
All rights reserved.

ATTACHED

ISBN
979-8-88504-638-1 *Paperback*
979-8-88504-956-6 *Kindle Ebook*
979-8-88504-843-9 *Digital Ebook*

To anyone who feels lost—you have all the answers inside, but you do not have to find them alone.

CONTENTS

PART 1 - IT IS WHAT IT IS	11
Chapter 1	13
Chapter 2	21
Chapter 3	27
Chapter 4	37
Chapter 5	45
Chapter 6	53
PART 2 - GIVE UP AND GIVE IN	59
Chapter 7	61
Chapter 8	69
Chapter 9	73
Chapter 10	83
Chapter 11	87
Chapter 12	101
Chapter 13	107
Chapter 14	121

Chapter 15	125
Chapter 16	135
Chapter 17	145
Chapter 18	151
Chapter 19	157
Chapter 20	167
PART 3 - ONE DAY AT A TIME	175
Chapter 21	177
Chapter 22	189
Chapter 23	197
Chapter 24	205
Chapter 25	215
Chapter 26	221
PART 4 - COME WHAT MAY	229
Chapter 27	231
Chapter 28	239
Chapter 29	245
Chapter 30	249
Chapter 31	255
Acknowledgments	263

Can you remember who you were before the world told you who you should be?

—LITTLE BOOKS OF WISDOM, CHARLES BUKOWSKI

IT IS WHAT IT IS

CHAPTER 1

I need to be in the woods to get away from that cabin and all it holds. Heat still leaches from my core after the fight I just had. I punctuate my words as I slam the heavy, dark oak cabin door in my sister's face. The reverberation will sting; it sure stung me as I let the knob fly.

Stalking away to my sanctuary of green trees and the misty morning, the argument I just finished reels through my head.

"She is dying, Maggie." The brutal and honest words had burst from my mouth.

"Ellie, there is still hope. We have to stay strong," Maggie tried to reason with me.

"She is dying. You know it, I know it, and Daddy knows it, too. That's why he's gone," I barked out to bring reality back to us both. We needed reality so we could figure out what to do. We needed to do something since sitting around and waiting was torture.

Maggie's light brows furrowed, her icy blue eyes widened, and her beautiful softness pissed me off when she chose optimism in a shitty situation. It especially grated at me when life slapped us in the face. Take your licks and move past it was my motto. The anticipation was worse than the sting of the hand

"At least I don't give up." Maggie used her hope to wound me.

"Give up? I don't give up but I also don't have any interest in powdering your ass just to make you *feel* better."

Being Maggie's younger sister by three years allowed the timing of our words and meanings to sting just enough. We were careful never to maim, but our spats always resulted in clean slashes from our tongues and the cadence to cut deep.

"I know she isn't well, Ellie, but you thinking the worst doesn't help." Maggie tried to take the higher road now that we did not have Momma's voice of reason between us.

"Isn't doing well? Look at her. She's disappearing right in front of us." Desperation cracked my words. As I turned my back, my eyes were stinging, and I reached for my rifle and thick, black, oversized jacket. My black wide-brimmed cowboy hat was already atop my head, so I pulled it down and the collar of my jacket up, walling off my sister. I needed space.

"Where are you going?" Maggie asked urgently.

"Out." I slammed the door behind me.

After playing the scene in my head, I mount my horse, Gunpowder, dig my heels in, and ride away from my problems. I was trying to outrun it all, if even just for a moment.

My momma's belly is full. She was due almost a week ago but the doctor from town believes the baby isn't ready. He says the baby is shutting down Momma's organs, and the only way to get it to stop is to deliver—and soon. But for some reason, that baby isn't ready to make its appearance yet. Not that I blamed the child. This world is cruel, and I could see the appeal of being in that woman's safe, nurturing body for as long as possible.

* * *

People say if you're a woman living in the mountains, you're either crazy or in love. I think Momma was both. My momma is now forty, and no one thought she could or should still deliver babies at her age. My parents had all but given up on this dream of more children—specifically the chances of producing a boy. Having babies and filling our house with them was all my momma ever wanted.

My momma, Annie, met my daddy, William, when he rode into town on a stolen train ticket traveling west through Montana in search of gold. They met at a dance hall. Daddy had walked right up to Momma in a flock of other blushing women like he was drawn to her. He was the moth to her flame.

His dreams of striking gold and heading west sounded like the adventure of a lifetime to my momma who had been stuffed up, primped, primed, and sent to boarding school. It helped that the adventure was attached to such an attractive face.

Momma recalls seeing my daddy for the first time. His deep dark brown eyes, broad shoulders, and smoldering presence were alluring and irresistible. Their eyes locked across the hall, and she remembered him walking right up to her, taking her hand without a word, never looking away, and they danced all night. Momma didn't care that her dance card was full. It was him and would always be him.

His fast talk and burning passion caused everyone to listen more closely. Momma once said he could charm a snake, but that was then. Somehow, though, life had snuffed that out.

Daddy was just as attracted to Momma's delicate features: light blond hair, kind blue eyes, and how she held her head high as any woman of means should. My daddy was also an opportunistic man, gunning for success, and saw that Annie was brought up as a lady. If he was going to be successful, he needed a woman from that world. Her light to his dark. They fell hard and fast and eloped two weeks after their first night together.

My daddy promised Momma that he would give her the life she deserved. He was going to strike gold and give her lots of babies. My momma just wanted babies and love. But daddy had come from poor dirt farmers, and they were cruel to him. From the way my momma told it, he had something to prove.

My grandad told Daddy he would end up just like him—a dirt farmer meant for nothin' more than to return to the dirt where he came from. My daddy labored from the age of four, and my grandad used him as a punching bag before eventually drinking himself to death. So Daddy sought to prove him wrong. He was going to strike gold, which was the only form of success that would prove it. My daddy never talked about it much, but I knew it drove him most days we were out panhandling for long hours.

So, my parents traveled farther out west to Washington following the rumor that gold was in these mountains, but no one had found it yet. My daddy always wanted his specific slice of the pie and did not want to share it with anyone. So he took my momma off the beaten path and settled on the northern border of Washington and Idaho Territory in 1864. There they made their claims on the land. Together, they built a house big enough to fill it with lots of children and love.

First came Maggie. She was not a disappointment. It did not matter what she was because chances were a boy was next; it made sense since most of their kin were men. Then I came, and that's when they started to worry. Daddy knew this mountain life was not easy for women, and now he had three of them to worry about. My parents continued to try for years but miscarriage after miscarriage continued to happen. That was twenty years ago, and to my daddy's disappointment, he never had a boy and had not struck gold—yet.

Since there were no big strikes of gold in these parts, with the completion of the Northern Pacific Railroad, other ways to make a living had popped up. Fur trading and mining for other precious metals were available, so more people flocked to the fast rough frontier.

The harsher and wilder folks were just naturally drawn to these parts. We lived out here with these "roughnecks" as they were called. Hunters, miners, fur traders, bootleggers, and outlaws became our neighbors. Mining was really the only occupation other than marriage for women, so only a few brave, crazy, or desperate women lived out here full time. The kids I grew up with were naturally rough too but I wasn't a lady like my sister so I didn't mind it.

Momma grew tired of waiting for Daddy to strike it rich, so out of necessity, she came up with her own idea of filling our big empty cabin another way. She convinced Daddy to open a shop for supplies. Our store then became the edge of civilization—the point that divides the vast wildness from humanity. Our shop is the last stop before the wildness swallows you up. It is the only place for the mountain dwellers to gather supplies. Otherwise, you had a half day's ride to town.

We avoided town as much as possible, and the "townies" preferred it that way too. When we had to make the reluctant trip ourselves, they parted like the Red Sea, as if they were afraid to catch something like the pox from us. Stares and whispers, hands on holsters, and mothers stepping in front of their babies were the only greetings we received. They made it known we were not welcome there. Not that I really cared. I never wanted to be there anyway.

Over time and as we grew, Maggie naturally took to helping my mother, and I followed my daddy. Daddy used the mountains to teach me about life and survival, and I would hang on to his every word, knowing full well that our survival depended on it. He brought me up like a boy, and that was fine by me.

He always said, "You were built for the mountains," when referring to my natural fit and tough nature.

Only just recently when my womanly curves began developing did people, particularly men, start treating me differently. My long dark hair resembled the dark brunette waves that graced my daddy's head, but my green eyes were my own. The mountain was my home, and I wasn't crazy or in love other than with the mountain and my family.

My momma tried to teach us etiquette and educated us both, but the pull of the wild always distracted me. Maggie always had a better chance at a proper life because of this. Everyone knew she would marry, be a good wife, and bear beautiful babies. Although she has not shown much interest in any particular man yet, that's just how it will be for her. Now, Maggie can handle the storefront and does so most of the time. Maggie is better with people and is just naturally softer in appearance and soul than I am, so it always made sense that she helped my momma.

For me, it's different. I never had any interest in being a wife or a mother. Daddy brought me up to survive in the harshness of the mountains but now I don't see them as harsh. The woods, rivers, and the rugged peaks are where I always feel most at home. The plan for my life was to protect my family, provide for them, strike gold like my daddy always wanted, and make sure Maggie got the life she deserved. It was that simple. Complicating it with love and expectations of taking over a household never fit me. That is my role—the end. It wasn't until Momma got pregnant and sick that I even considered worrying that my plans were flawed.

* * *

My daddy is not well, either, and I am not ready to do this alone. He lost his drive for anything now that Momma is so ill. As she fails, he fails. He is drunk all the time and no longer even cares about the hunt for gold. I am getting worried that if Momma doesn't make it, the best parts of Daddy will go with her.

Focus now. Slowing Gunpowder, we walk along for a ways to calm my senses. I have hunted plenty of times alone. As we meander along a game trail, I check my trap closest to our cabin, not surprised it has ensnared a rabbit, already dead. Rabbits are a good source of protein, but they do not have enough fat on them to eat by themselves for long periods of time.

The doctor said to find other game and try and get Momma to eat it so her body doesn't have to work so hard to process it. I am hoping for a fat deer this time of year. The paleness and lifelessness of the limp rabbit in my hand reminds me of Momma's blanched face this morning. It sends a pang violently to my guts.

My life is beginning to crumble. All I hold dear is slipping through my fingers like dry sand. The more I squeeze, the quicker I lose it. I need to save what's left of my family if the worst happens, and after this morning, I think the worst is coming. What if all I have, all I am, no longer existed? That would leave just me, and just me scares the *shit* out of me.

"Stop thinking like that," I say to myself out loud and shake my head, but I can't. I've seen enough failing animals.

Momma, the one who's held us all stitched together, is fraying like a rope on its last threads.

I dismount Gunpowder and allow him to graze on some soft greens. Lowering my knee to the ground, my body supports my weight. I don't have to stay there long.

As I raise my awareness, focusing my senses to distract myself from the worry, a large buck steps obliviously into my view. Breathing out steadily, I fire my rifle. My bullet lands in his chest. He attempts to sprint away from the pain and noise, which have already fatally wounded him. His muscled body makes it up the hillside and then drops. To my relief, he rolls down the hill, back to where my bullet initially pierced him.

Setting my jaw to field dressing gave my hands something to do for over an hour. As I slash through the warm flesh, flitting relief washes over me, knowing this kill will provide for our whole family for the rest of the week. A sigh escapes my lips as I tie the buck to Gunpowder.

I can now stay close to home, I thought tiredly. Brushing my hair out of my face and then pulling my leather black hat down further over my brow, I begin the trek home.

CHAPTER 2

The hairs on the back of my neck lift as I enter the cabin. I discard my kill on the floor, not worrying about the bloody mess it will leave. Instinctively I know it's time. I can hear the rough jagged inhale and rapidly pursed exhale clearly from where I stand. Each breath entwined with a painful whimper comes from my momma, and it breaks my heart.

My sister's murmuring soft voice echoes reassurance following the haggard sounds coming from the back of the cabin in my parents' room. A stale tension fills the space, the tang of copper hanging in the air that I know is coming from her.

From the front door, I cross the large room where our shop takes up most of the space and move past the kitchen on the right. My steps take me directly to the back long, dark hallway, which amplifies Momma's cries. I make quick time past the room I share with my sister and sprint to my parents' door that hovers ajar. The flickering candlelight throws shadows up the wall in an ominous hue.

The plank just outside their room, ever loose, creeks under my feet and alerts Maggie of my presence. Maggie's light brown hair is pinned up, indicating she is ready to work. She is positioned below my momma's legs and wipes the blood away.

"There shouldn't be that much blood, Maggie." My voice is hollow and flat, as I take in the heaps of saturated rags that already litter the wooden planks around the floor at my sister's feet.

Maggie's blue eyes are intense as she clips out, "I know."

"Where is Daddy?" I ask.

"I sent him to get the doctor." The doctor worked in town and could only be reached in a half a day's ride on a good day. He would be too late, and Maggie knew this too.

Momma is sallow, yellow, and thinner than she should be. I see the light in her eyes flicker for a moment, and my heart nearly stops. Rushing over to the bedside, needing to do something, I grab her dainty, frail, clammy hand in mine. Momma turns her head to face me, and her gaze softens. With vacant but peaceful eyes, she looks toward me but is miles away.

"Momma, you gotta hold on, you hear me? Maggie and I need you. Daddy needs you." It comes out more brutally than I intend.

She reaches for me with her other hand and cups my face.

"You will take care of them. Won't you?" Momma whispers through cracked lips.

"I won't need to because they'll have you. Don't you leave us," I warn her.

She doesn't acknowledge my warning, and her head drifts back to the saturated sweaty pillow. Holding her own head up is too much of a burden now. Releasing my face, she cringes through a cramp as it racks her tiny body, and she squeezes my hand with barely any strength.

Maggie exclaims, "The head is out!" One of her hands is holding the tiny skull while the other is preparing to catch the rest.

Briefly craning my neck, I look down but regret it immediately. I zero in only on the blood, so much blood.

Momma pushes and grunts, no screaming like I imagined. Her strength and determination are focused only on birthing her child. Sweat rolls down her temples. The blond hair around the nape of her neck curls and plasters to her.

"Okay, Momma, now you need to push… hard. *Now*," Maggie says confidently, definitively.

Their eyes connect, and their bond clicks into place. Momma's abdomen contracts and she grunts out a guttural feral sound, one an animal makes right before their last breath.

Maggie reacts to the release and catches the wet crying human as it falls from Momma.

"It's a girl," Maggie whispers, her eyes glistening as she wraps our baby sister in the light blue and yellow quilted blanket she had made weeks ago just for this moment.

Then the flood gates burst. Blood slides in a constant gush from Momma. I hold her hand and watch as my sister tries to respond.

Maggie lays our screaming sister on the floor and hopelessly applies pressure with a towel. The light blue of the fabric becomes the color of a dark night instantly, saturated and useless. Too much blood continues to pour from her.

I hear myself scream, "Momma, you stop this. Stop it right now."

Maggie grabs yet another blanket to add more pressure, discarding the useless saturated one next to the other failed limp rags surrounding her feet. Our eyes meet in unison, and dread mirrors back at me.

The faint grip in my palm releases, signaling it is done holding on, no longer doing its part to stay connected. I grasp her hand tighter, willing and wanting a reciprocal squeeze, but it never comes. The light from her eyes dims and snuffs out completely seconds later. Momma is gone.

The front door to the cabin bangs hard against the wall and makes us all jump. Seconds later, Daddy rushes in alone. He doesn't have the doctor. His eyes search his lifeless wife for any movement.

He pushes past Maggie and me and grabs Momma's face.

"Annie? Annie? No, baby, no. You can't leave me." His tears boil over the rims of his wide frantic eyes, and his brows crumple in defeat.

"Oh, Annie." Daddy rocks her lifeless body, pulling her closer and onto his lap, swaying with his sobs. His lumbering square body convulses, and I can see the pain rippling tension across his broad shoulders with every breath.

Maggie picks up our screaming sister and tears fall down her cheeks in silent streams. Her face is frozen. She holds our baby sister in her arms but does not move. My tears spill over in a hot gush. Even our baby sister knows there's nothing else to do but cry as she continues to wail loudly.

The scene shatters my heart. I've never seen Daddy cry and this makes my vision blur completely until I have to look away. Sobs rack my body in unison with his violent cries.

"Get out," he growls.

"Daddy, no. We need to stick together." I reach for his shoulder, touching it lightly and attempting to offer comfort.

"Get *out!*" he screams.

Jumping, I pull my hand away as if I'd just touched the hot stove.

Covering my mouth with the back of my hand, the same one that attempted to comfort my broken father moments ago, I choke back my tears.

Stepping away quickly, I grab Maggie, who is still frozen in place, and guide her to the sofa by the fire in the big room connected to the shop. She continues to hold our now quiet baby sister in her arms. I wrap my arms around Maggie's thin shoulders as we sit and rock together. Sobs turn to chokes, and then sniffles turn to silence as we stare into the flames licking the glass of the stove, hypnotic and comforting. We wince occasionally at Daddy's wails thundering down the hall.

Momma's left us with the remains of a man—one who hasn't gotten anything he wanted out of life. I've seen glimpses of that man but hid it from the rest of my family the best I could over the years, trying to protect him and them from his darkness. I don't know what I'll do, though, if darkness is all that is left.

CHAPTER 3

The quiet haunting our cabin is deafening. A week's passed since we lost Momma, and her absence punches a gaping hole in our lives. We have no words for the grief weighing down on us, so silence consumes us.

Everyone loved Momma, and it is obvious. We find extra meat, supplies, and meals on the porch or they are hand-delivered with condolences. Even the bootleggers leave a pallet of moonshine so we have enough medicine to numb the ice pick pain stabbing our hearts. Life is just less sunny without our momma in it.

After her death, Daddy searches to find the perfect spot for his wife. The intensity in his focus and direction releases some of the jaw-clenching tension I've been holding for him. Maybe he won't drop into the pit of despair.

Hanging on to this hope gives me the strength to shoulder the weight of our future. Together, we can power through this. I am here for him. I know him better than anyone, and he's hurting. I ignored the extra moonshine he drank to limp through these last few weeks. God knows I indulge with him when no one is looking. I even ignore the nights I have to carry-drag him from the tavern—so drunk he can't stand. This is part of him getting over the loss of our mother. *We will get through this,* I reassure myself over and over.

He chooses a soft meadow knoll with a view of the valley to dig her grave. We dig that hole silently together—drunk on liquor and determination. Wiping away angry hot tears, smearing soil across our faces into muddy masks, ignoring each other's sniffs and coughs, we hide our sorrow. It drives us harder to get the terrible job done.

* * *

The ceremony is a blur. A moment of clarity and appreciation shakes me from my trance when I scan the room behind us. Up front and off to the right are Graham and his father Daniel Parson. They've been not only our business partners but our friends over the years, even though they are technically townies. The Parson men had a way of fitting in wherever they needed to. Being mercantile and tradesmen requires interactions with all walks of life. Striking a deal with a banker one day and then an outlaw the next, resulting in a skillful two-step only Graham and his father seemed to know how to balance with rhythmic ease. Being on the road between towns on trading trips seems to suggest that traversing the wilderness is part of their job.

Their gift of managing people, riding, shooting, and hunting has made them downright successful. Some of the mountain folk have even accepted them—sometimes offering them a drink or showing them the local secret spots. Others never warmed up to the Parson men since they were not truly one of us. I hadn't held this against him since we were kids. Graham had proved to me he could keep up long ago.

Still choking me up, I recall Graham's embrace before the ceremony. He is warm and strong; it almost makes me collapse into a heap of tears and deep sorrow. But I know if I let this part of me out, I won't be able to wind it back up or keep it together in the way my family needs. I cut the embrace short and pull back for protection. The responsibilities and traditions demand too much of my attention to allow myself to unravel.

Keep it together, Ellie, I warn myself.

Outlaws and bootleggers fill most of the middle section. Logan Clancy and his gang, even Tricia, are here. They make it through the ceremony by sneaking swigs from their pocket flasks. Gray smoke continuously curls above their heads as they chain-smoke tobacco. I don't consider Logan or Tricia a friend, but growing up and surviving the mountains together has earned a certain level of understanding and respect. We have a sense of deep belonging—an unspoken badge of honor and merit among us.

We are all survivors, though. Each person paying their respects carries at least one pistol on their hip. Multiple knives peek out of boots while more hide in sleeves and corsets. Weapons are always concealed but ready and available. If you wrong them, blood is still shed. After the pomp and circumstance, things will go back to normal.

The only person who surprised me was the old mountain woman, Aponi, and her gray wolf, Fin, who stand respectfully in the back decorated in turquoise and leather. Her golden honey-brown eyes meet my green ones just as the ceremony ends. Her chin tips down at me in acknowledgment before she leaves. I never saw Momma and her exchange much more than the transactional pleasantries of a deal, but apparently, my momma made an impression even then.

We bury Momma in a beautiful wooden coffin Daddy hand-made with her name torched across it. A simple wooden cross marks her spot.

* * *

Everyone returns to normal life once Momma is in the ground, except Daddy, who just stops living. He stumbles to bed and only gets up for more alcohol or to relieve himself.

I can feel the spite and anger start to reverberate from his room, but his fatigue and sorrow keep it contained, locked behind the door in his cave, which stinks of sadness, alcohol, and salt.

As we run out of the liquid keeping Daddy sedated, I worry about what will come next. Should I keep him in a stupor or force him out? He needs to resurface sooner or later, but I don't know if that would be better than this shell of a human in front of me. Without it, he will have to face the reality of three girls without a momma.

"Maggie, he hasn't been out of bed for days," I push out flatly.

"He is hurting, El. Leave him alone. He will get up soon," she replies as she rocks our baby sister, who is sleeping in her naturally capable arms.

"I know he's hurting. We all are. That doesn't mean we stop living, you know?" I try to hide the desperation crawling up from my gut.

"I know. I know, but sometimes people need some time. He needs time, El." Maggie seems to say this to me and herself.

"He needs to take care of his family," I huff out under my breath.

If he doesn't help out, the responsibility of protecting and providing will fall on me, and I'm not sure I'm ready to do it alone. Besides, he needs something to do, to live for. Aren't we enough for him to choose to get out of that God-damned bed?

"I need to go out hunting, Mags. Do you think you'll be okay?" The unspoken question is, *Will you be okay here alone if he wakes up?* We both know what I mean.

When he runs out of booze, things could get ugly. Given the extent of his anger and hurt, I don't know *when* he's going to erupt but I need to be here *when* he does.

Maggie considers this. "We will be okay. Just don't go too far out, all right?" Her voice trembles slightly; I know she counts on me to wrangle Daddy's anger the way I always do.

He has never hit Maggie but I'm not so sure it isn't in him now. She is a strong woman, also raised in these mountains, but she's been protected from some of it. I've made sure of that.

Our eyes connect and we communicate a knowing that does not need words. I nod and collect my hunting rifle and gear. Dressed in brown leather pants, I shoulder on my jacket and look at Maggie in her pale white and blue floor-length dress; her softness seems more exposed as she holds our baby sister in her arms.

"I will stay close and hunt," I reassure us both as I continue to get ready. "If something goes wrong, fire twice with your pistol. You hear?"

She nods as she locates her pistol and secures it to her belt.

My shoulders drop a little once she has the weapon close to her. Resigning to stay close, I exit the cabin with determination. I'll make a point to stop by the bootleggers or the saloon to pick up another crate of moonshine just in case. I just can't decide what would be worse.

Leaving the cabin is harder than it has ever been but I haven't hunted since the funeral, and we have already eaten all the premade meals. The early crisp morning bites at my nose as I pull my leather jacket up around my ears. I'm wearing my hunting leathers, and the fluid motion of my muscles back in action satisfies the stagnation of the last three weeks.

My senses ease from being in the woods like a drink of crisp water cooling me on a hot summer day. The songs of the birds' melodies meander to my ears in a lazy contented way. The quivering leaves dancing with the breeze and the smell of the fresh pine boughs fill my nostrils.

Inhaling deeply settles my nerves a bit more. I'm glad to get away from the cabin; its emotion and tension take up all the space. I can't help my dripping guilt, though. Maggie never gets away from home. I can see why she would complain about how it always feels too small—even though it is bigger than any other cabin within twenty miles.

My heartbeat is now steady. The reprieve from my pain is liberating. My spirits lift, and the release is intoxicating. Doing a job, this job of protecting my family and providing for them is all I know. This is what I'm made for.

I pick up a handful of dried leaves and crumple them in the wind. My scent is traveling to the east, so I follow it and then turn around, posting up against a tree. Lying down, I position myself just outside of the open field where I know the game chooses to feast on soft new grass.

My ears perk up, and I'm on alert for any subtle sound. I'm in my element. I lie there for a long time, observing the different greens contrasting against the mountainside as it darkens with the elevation from the cold winter still touching its foliage. I hear the hot puff from the elk first and then see her step into the clearing with a graceful saunter. This will be a quiet and successful hunt.

I allow myself to savor the anticipation before I pull the trigger. Sucking in my breath, I pause just long enough to ride the escape a moment longer. Letting out my breath, I squeeze the trigger and embrace the kick from my rifle into my shoulder; life is coursing through me.

My kill is quick and the cow drops hard, dead on impact. Quickly, I dress and pack her neatly onto Gunpowder. As we ride back with a quick gallop, I am lighter than I have been in weeks. The tightness in my chest loosens knowing I am quick, efficient, and responsible.

* * *

"Daddy, it's time to get out of bed," I finally demand after several more days. I've had enough of this. I lift the quilt off of him. It's been over a month now of watching him fester in between the sheets of their bed. I'm done with this phase. He needs to get up and move.

He does not respond, just grumbles and rolls his back to me and onto Momma's side of the bed. Intently, I watch his body for any movement, any response.

"You need to take care of this family like you promised you would. For Momma."

I am not above using guilt, force, or manipulation. He is not well and needs to get up. He no longer knows what is best for him, but I do. I will use any form of coercion I need to move him. The gloves are off.

"You brought us out here now you need to take care of us," I plead with him.

Again no response.

"You have a new baby girl who needs a daddy. She needs a name. You need to hold her, for God's sake." Next, I turn to guilt and shame.

His shoulders shift in muted response. He rolls over to his back, his greasy hair smashing against the pillow, and disgust flashes across my mind. My lip pulls up at him.

"I got no name for that devil who took your momma away from me," he snarls.

At least I got a response out of him, I muse.

"That baby did not choose to come into this world on her own. You and Momma brought her here." I use my opening to rouse any sort of life back into this man. Even anger is better than this shell of apathy. "Momma wanted her. That needs to be enough for you to respect her wishes and take care of her baby. For God's sake, name her, or we will—after Momma." My chin juts out with the challenge.

His dark brown eyes flare with heat. Good. At least I'm finally getting something out of him.

"She will not have my Annie's name," he barks out at me as he pushes to his forearms and makes to get up.

"Then you better name her something else!" This is working.

"I don't give a damn what you name her just not Annie." His feet touch the floor.

Finally, a wave of relief washes over me. He is unsteady on his own two feet, but at least he is up. I hand him the flask I now carry around. He snatches it from my hands. Kicking his head back, he downs the liquid quickly and hands it back to me only because my fingers remained there, waiting the whole time. He could only have a little.

"At least you have *one* redeeming quality," he mutters.

Following him out of his room, I kept an eye on Maggie and the baby.

Maggie eyes Daddy, too. Stepping a foot closer, she turns our baby sister's face toward him. The baby is in a pleasant mood, just after a feeding. She smiles broadly and toothlessly at him. His eyes darken and glisten in unison.

"Her name is Lottie." His voice hitches. Slinging on his coat, he flings the door open, stalks through it, and then slams it shut. The windows rattle after him.

"At least he is finally out of bed," I say to Maggie.

She looks at our little sister, Lottie, swaddled in her arms.

"Anger might just get him out of this. Thank you, Ellie." Maggie sways with Lottie.

"For what?"

"For being brave enough to care."

I do care. I care so much about this family I'd do anything for them. I love that man so much even though he is as easy to love as a defensive porcupine. Daddy and I understand each other in a way no one else seems to. Prodding his stubbornness like an unruly bull, I use a hot poker to motivate him. It's what will work for him.

Now that he's up, we can start to live life without Momma. Nothing is worse than numbness and festering.

CHAPTER 4

I tie Gunpowder's thick leather reins to the saloon pole a little too harshly and then stalk to its entrance. Getting Daddy out of bed initially felt like a successful feat, at least a step in the right direction—until retrieving him from this shit hole became a daily task. Prostitutes stand out front, and the one I despise the most is leaning her voluptuous body over to block the entrance—Tricia. I glare at her.

She curls her rosy full lips into a sweet vicious smile. "Hey, Ellie, lookin' for your daddy?" Her voice is a taunting octave dripping with insinuation.

Slitting my eyes, I don't respond. I do not have the energy for her tonight. I try to make it past her without clawing at the string she is obviously trying to dangle in my face.

Tricia sways her full hips and then braces her tightly tressed-up corseted body directly in the doorway with her arms, looking down her delicate button nose at me; she is not moving without a confrontation. She is known for her talents of the night, but she also runs with Logan Clancy and his gang. She is a good shot and has a proclivity for stirring up trouble; she could be deadly if she wanted to.

"Well, is he in there, Trish?" I ask pointedly.

"I'm not entirely sure. I just got here. I know he was here last night."

Rolling my eyes, I try again to push past her.

"He seemed lonely last night, so I kept him company," Tricia tweets out just as I am about to pass her.

We had grown up together, so she knows exactly how to press my buttons. We're always at each other's throats with our equally sharp tongues—mainly because Logan has always shown an interest in me and not her. Not that I have any time for him, especially now, but she hates that his gaze and attention always drift my way. I know it, she knows it, and we both use it against each other. We compete at everything.

"I'm sure he did since your specialty is to lure broken, easy prey. I figured you'd outgrow that by now and want something more challenging. I reckon effort will never be one of your strong suits. Picking the low-hanging fruit? Typical," I say, trying yet again to dismiss her.

Her hand grabs my arm as she steps in closer, jutting her full breasts into my shoulder. Her breath hits my ear, warm and seductive. "The low-hanging fruit is the sweetest and easiest to bruise." She licks my ear with the tip of her sharp tongue, and a wicked smile whisks across her lips.

Red-hot rage shoots through me and my guts twist into my throat. Shoving her against the tavern wall, I pin her with my forearm, warning her I could easily choke that ivory neck. We are inches apart, nose to nose. Her eyes are wide with the challenge as our chests touch, and our breathing is heavy.

We both glance down, noticing the opposing points of our knives are poised just above the other's abdomen. A flicker of respect and admiration is there but dissolves quickly; it isn't the first time we had pointed weapons at each other and likely won't be the last.

"Whoa, ladies, please." Logan's tall body exits the saloon swiftly. The wood swinging doors clap and the piano music from inside follows him. He towers next to us, placing a rough and large hand on both of our tense shoulders.

Tricia and I keep our gazes locked.

Logan moves his hands from our shoulders to the leather hilts on our knives, drawing them away from the delicate flesh they threaten to pierce.

"We are short on pretty women in these parts. I don't understand why the prettiest two around can't ever seem to get along." His voice, deep and rugged, drawls out of his handsome chiseled jaw.

He presses us away, decompressing the tension with the strength of his body. We both sheathe our knives, and I back away a few more steps.

Never turn your back on a snake, I think.

Tricia continues to lean into the wall, lifting one of her legs so we can see the white full thighs and muscles supporting her. She grabs Logan by the coat and pulls him into her. His hand grasps the outside of her exposed flesh.

"Logan, baby, we were just playing. Ellie and I go way back. We would never really hurt each other, *physically*." Emphasis on the physical part; the mental warfare is on.

"Tricia, you are causing extra trouble today. Leave poor Ellie alone. She has enough to deal with." His voice rings in my ears as patronizing. Turning my body to push through the wooden dark mahogany swinging doors, I want to get away from both of them.

Tricia's full rosy bottom lip pouts out. "That's why I took such good care of her daddy last night."

Logan is fully between us in an instant, and he uses his unoccupied hand to push me inside before I can draw blood. I am strong but damn him, he is stronger. I stumble into the saloon's dark hall and glare over my shoulder. Tricia blows me a kiss as I fling my middle finger into the air.

Sitting at the poker table under the dingy candle lantern is my daddy. He has a showgirl wearing corsets and heels perched on his lap. Her bottom hangs over his leg, and his hand stays on her low back just above the white ruffles covering her round cheeks. When Momma was alive, he would have verbalized his appreciation for these women. Now, he is ready to indulge in the taste and the feel of them too, I guess. I imagine it is a salve to soothe his loneliness and broken heart. I don't blame him but I wish he had waited a bit longer.

He places his cards down on the rough splintered table to polish off his drink and then spanks the showgirl, Loretta, swiftly. As he hands her the glass, he bellows, "Another one, honey, and keep 'em comin'."

Loretta jumps up, tips her chin at me, and then diverts her eyes quickly down and away. Loretta is quiet and shy, and men love her because of it. I don't fault her for this or her profession; she is just trying to survive the harsh mountains in a man's world. We're all playing a role.

Daddy's eyelids droop over glassy eyes, and I can see his luck is poor. He is a piss-poor gambler and drinker, apparently. The other four men around the table track Daddy with viciousness. They're predators toying with their prey.

"Looks like you boys did it again," I say, through my clenched teeth.

This is not the first time I had to drag Daddy from this burned-up and washed-out table. Knowing by now how this will end, I try to line my pockets with enough money to bail him out, but this time looks worse.

"Shut up, Ellie, I'm havin' a comeback," Daddy slurs and pulls his cards close to his nose. He has to close one eye to see straight.

Shiiiit, I need to get him out of here.

"Honey, let him play. He's a big boy." His greasy, black-haired opponent doesn't look at me while he settles in his chair confidently.

Loretta returns with the glass of brown liquor just the way Daddy orders it—straight and harsh. I snatch it from her polished fingers before she is able to give it to him, and toss it down the back of my throat.

"Hey, that's mine!" He reaches for the glass I'd already slammed down, his movement slow and clumsy.

"Not anymore." Flat sarcasm laces my words. I am already tired of this place and everyone in it.

"You goin' to let your daughter talk to you like that?" the man across the table chortles.

"You must be new 'round here." Logan steps in next to me and slides his arm around my shoulders. "Ellie has venom on her tongue and fire in her heart. It's what we love about her."

Logan is trying to smooth things over for me but I don't want his or anyone else's help. He is sticking his nose into my business when I didn't want it. Shrugging him off, I walk closer to the table. I snatch my daddy's cards from his hands and throw them down. *He has nothin'.*

His eyes drift to mine but he can't focus. Stupidly, he smiles at me. It's embarrassing but he's still my daddy and my heart falters at the loyalty I have for him.

Setting my jaw and lips in a tight line, I bark out, "How much does he owe?" I don't lose eye contact with the drunken mess before me.

"He owes us his gun and fifty dollars." The man with the most chips smiles over his hand of cards; smoke puffs out as he talks.

I throw down all the money I had in my pockets and then pull Daddy's gun from his holster and slam it on the table. The metal gleaming barrel points at the man's chest. Leaning over the table, my finger grips the trigger as I reply, "That's forty dollars and his gun. It's all I have."

The man lays his dirty hand on mine and then caresses my trigger finger. "I believe I said fifty dollars, honey."

"Call me honey one more time," I warn, as I click back the hammer.

He rips his hand back and throws both hands in the air in surrender, sensing I mean it. "Your Paw still owes us ten dollars. How we gonna settle this?" He and I know people around these parts paid their debts in money, gold, or flesh.

Logan slides the difference onto the table. I shake my head and roll my eyes before nodding a reluctant thanks. He knows I'm good for it.

"Thank you kindly." The man swipes his winnings and then tips his hat at me.

By now, Daddy is passed out heavily on the table, letting me fight his battles with no remorse. Lowering down to where his body lays slumped over, I lift him. Logan goes to the other side and helps me drag his limp body to Gunpowder.

Slinging him over the horse is not easy, which is the only reason I accept Logan's help again.

I grunt out a curt, "Thanks."

"Anytime, El. You know I'm here for you." He reaches for my cheek with his hand—the same hand that squeezed Tricia's thigh. I try and back away, attempting to shut him out, but he takes a step closer, closing the space between us.

"Hey, if you ever need to blow off some steam, I could take your mind off all this. You'll forget it all—at least for a few hours." His hazel eyes flash with evocative intent.

He also knows how to get my goat; we too grew up together and have played this carnal dance and tease since we both hit puberty. I know drinking from that pool will make me as sick as drinking from a warm shallow puddle in the summer. Quenching my thirst comes at its own cost. We still flirt with the balance, though, much like when we were kids playing next to cliffs, shoving each other over the edge and into the water below.

"A few minutes is more like it, I imagine," I joust back.

He drops his hand and unties the reins, keeping them just out of my reach. "We could time ourselves and see who wins that bet," he says as his eyes glint at me.

"The day we see how that plays out is the day you know I've given up."

He motions to my daddy. "Give it up, Ellie. You are one of us. You come by it honestly."

Bristling at this, I snatch the leathers from his hand and guide Gunpowder away from this wretched place.

I know Logan is watching my backside as I walk away. I sway my hips a bit more to tease him—wanting to have the last blow. Competition is a nasty habit of mine.

Starting the walk home, I take in my daddy's slack drooling face. I envy the relief he is getting from oblivion. The reality I'm enduring, choosing to not be numb with vices, is getting more and more difficult to handle. I'm starting to tire of doing the right thing—of being the voice of reason and pulling him out of it all. He is the parent after all. Why am I babysitting him?

I start to think he has something figured out that I don't. Maybe all of them do. Tricia, Logan, Loretta, the gamblers, bootleggers—all of them have something I don't... freedom. I want a break, to release the crushing weight of responsibility and guilt I carry around with me, but I know I can't. If I don't hold it together for my sisters now, who will?

I shove those thoughts away and take my drunk daddy back to our house to tuck him in for another blissfully oblivious night.

CHAPTER 5

"Annie."

My mother's name whispers across my consciousness. Her sweet soft features blur together at first and then become a fully formed figure.

Annie, the woman who taught me to read. The one who taught me kindness and manners, who is warm and loved by all.

"Annie." I hear her name again and see her blue eyes like the spring sky. She smiles sweetly at me.

Moving closer to her, I want to see what she is holding so gently, tenderly. She looks down at her arms and there nestles our little sister, Lottie.

I hurry to her. A sense of urgency propels my steps. It feels as if I have forever and only a moment left with her.

"Annie." My mother's elegant neck snaps up and the white of her eyes expands. My heart quickens as I read the worry painted across her face.

"Annie." The name transforms from a soft caress to a sharp demand.

"*Annie!*" My reality comes stampeding through sweet dreams in the gruffness of Daddy's voice.

My eyes flash open. It is either late night or early morning.

Earlier that evening, I decided to let Daddy stay out. I had pulled, coaxed, and carried him from that saloon five times in the last week, and he continued to crawl back there every night and sometimes all day. It's been six months since Momma died, and I can't continue to baby him and take care of my sisters.

Last night was the most peaceful night we'd had in a long time. Maggie made dinner, and I played with Lottie. Lottie was now sitting up and supporting herself on her hands and knees. I placed the cloth doll Maggie made out of my mother's handkerchief just out of her reach, hoping to coax her into a crawl.

We had all climbed into bed together, and Maggie's reading put us to sleep. We slept in the same room even though our parents' room was mostly vacant. It was still our daddy's room.

"Anniiiieeee," Daddy continues to scream, searching for a woman who would not and could not answer his cries.

Outside the window, his dark figure stumbles in a lazy curve with a wide gait toward the cabin. He takes a few more unsteady steps and loses his footing completely, falling face-first into the dirt.

Maggie stirs and finally wakes up. "I will go deal with him," she says sleepily, still waking up.

"No, you won't." My feet touch the cold floor. My boots are next to the bed for this reason, and I shove my bare feet into their thick warn leather.

"Ellie, let me do it," Maggie protests from the bed.

"I got him. You watch Lottie. If she wakes up, none of us will get any rest." I am now fully alert as I speak over my shoulder and leave our room.

My coat is on the hook but I don't need it since the nights are so much warmer now. It is finally summer.

White stars poke through the inky black sky, and the nearly full moon illuminates my way. Translucent clouds move rapidly across it as the cool night air caresses my skin. It would be welcoming if I didn't have to deal with the mess rooting around in front of me.

Vomit and booze permeate from him and it singes my nostrils and my nerves.

"Annie?" His dark hollow eyes peer up at my face in hopeful earnestness. In his haze, it looks like he is trying to figure out if I am his Annie. Disappointment washes over his face as the recognition of mine sets in.

"Where is your momma?" he snaps at me.

Should I lie to him or just tell him the truth? Knowing full well that reason is beyond this man currently, I decided to go with reality tonight. Lord knows if it doesn't end well this time, I'll have another night to try it differently.

"Momma isn't here anymore. Momma is dead. Remember?" I'm carefully keeping my distance and assessing whether he's in a swinging mood.

He crawls to me, and even this primitive motion sends him wobbling.

"If she's dead, why the fuck am I still here?" he slurs and spits at the same time.

My mind scrambles for an answer to a question I've asked myself many times, but I don't have one.

"I don't know." Direct and to the point, I try to give him something to do to distract him. "But you need to get inside and go to bed. Sleep it off, all right?" Tentatively I take a few steps closer.

His head lolls back and forth. It's apparently too heavy, and he rests his forehead on the ground. He grumbles out something inaudible.

"What was that?" I snap, my annoyance building.

"I never should've brought her here. Now she's dead, gone, and I have nothin'. I am nothin'. Dirt, like my pa always said. No gold, no wife, and three daughters."

"Stop feeling sorry for yourself, you sorry sonofabitch, and get up!" I'm biting this out to protect myself from the last blow.

But he can't and he won't. In this moment, I know this man has given up; he's broken. He is gone. His body flops limp, sending his face back into the dirt. He passes out and seems lifeless other than the deep snores reverberating from his hollow chest.

Flipping him over, I muscle myself under his armpits, a hold I have mastered at this point. I am able to get him to the porch but I need help. Maggie is waiting at the door for her part in this routine. Lifting his dirty boots and legs, I hoist him up over the edge of the porch.

"He is pissing himself," Maggie notices with disgust.

Maggie never cusses—even this word is usually too vulgar for her. The edge and cut in her voice say what we were both thinking. We are tired of this and can't believe he has let himself go this much.

"Goddamn it!" Losing my grip, I drop his upper body onto the floor. His head bounces off the wood plank porch step with a *tha-thunk.*

My butt cushions my fall. Maggie loses her grip and drops his legs too. Our eyes survey his face for any sign of consciousness, but he sleeps on.

Bookending my passed-out father, we look at each other and start to laugh.

Uncontrollable belts of laughter rack us both. Leaning back on the heel of one hand, I clutch my side and just let it all out. The laughter dissolves from hysterical gayety to boiling hot anger quickly. On my hands and knees, I spring to my feet and kick him hard in the shoulder. Again, nothing.

Tears stream down my sneering face, and Maggie is taking me in. My anger is crippling. I want to kick him over and over. I want to scream at him. I want him to choose to get up.

Maggie walks over to me and firmly grabs both of my shoulders. "Let's leave him here for the night."

This seems too kind. I want to take him back outside and leave him there for the wolves and beasts to get him, but I don't want Maggie to know how vindictive I really am. So I say nothing.

Maggie grabs a blanket and lays it over him before returning with a pillow. She lifts his head and places the softness under it. He settles in.

My sister is so much better than I am. She has kindness in her heart as our momma had. I can't muster this level of kindness, and the darkness starts to creep up in my gut and boil there. The monster is starting to stir inside of me, but I coax it back down into submission. I have to stay good for my sisters.

Stalking into our room, I kick my boots off, rip the covers back, and plop into bed. Maggie follows me, shuts the door, and locks it for good measure. The fact that she needs to lock it in the first place stokes the flames in my chest like dry leaves. I am not sure I can maintain this composure much longer. As I fight to go back to sleep, tossing and turning in bed, for some reason the memory of when my first chicken stopped laying eggs appears.

* * *

When I was six, I went out to collect eggs for the morning. Caring for the chickens had become my first true outside chore, and I reveled in it. I skipped up to the chicken coop but my little tummy flipped when I looked under Harriett, my very first chicken's fat feathered bottom. Again, there were no eggs.

Initially, I had confided in Daddy because I was worried about my pet. I told him Harriett stopped producing eggs, thinking he might know how to fix her.

He'd threatened, "If she doesn't start laying eggs, she ain't worth keepin'."

So for weeks, I had covered for her and lied to Daddy—now fearful for her life.

Giving her extra pets and corn, I tried to give her more attention, urging her to lay more eggs.

When he wasn't looking, I would take an egg from one of the other hens and put it in Harriett's count. Eventually, he caught on. I got a whippin' for lyin' to him, and he was now watching more closely.

I slowly filled my basket one morning and took my time back to the kitchen. Quietly, I slid the basket of eggs on the counter, hoping he wouldn't ask.

"Any eggs from Harriett?" he asked over the brim of a steaming coffee mug.

My heart dropped. I looked at the ground and grumbled out, "No."

He pushed himself away from the counter and walked over to me.

"Ellie, if she ain't givin' us eggs, she ain't welcome here anymore." He looked at me and waited until our eyes met.

"This is part of taking care of chickens, and if they stop laying eggs, they become our food."

My whole body began to shake. "Harriett is my friend. I raised her and protected her. She trusts me."

"And now you are going to kill her so we can save feed for the other chickens. The feed costs money, and if she ain't contributin', she ain't worth nothin'," he said. Worthiness came from production is what he meant.

"I will not kill her." I made my tiny frame as big as it could be.

He grabbed my wrist and pulled me outside; I struggled against his strength and dug my feet in the dirt. My heart pounded in my ears, and red-hot tears burned the lining of my eyes.

He pulled me along with no effort and said through gritted teeth, "This is part of survivin' out here. You need to learn this right here and now, girl. Freeloaders ain't got no place here."

He pulled me to his ax and yanked it from the wood wedge. My eyes widened, and I knew what he meant to do. I backed away toward my hens and saw them waddle up to me as I'd trained them to do. Harriett was the first to reach me.

These were *my* chickens, *my* girls.

I turned and ran at them so they would fly off—my last attempt at saving Harriett. They scattered, and Daddy stalked off in the direction of Harriett. He took two long strides and grabbed her by her white feathered neck. He tucked her under his arm, pinning her wings down. He shoved the heavy ax at my chest, but I pushed it away and let it hit the ground. Then I looked up at him, silently pleading with my tear-streaked face. *Please don't make me do this.*

He lifted his lip and grabbed Harriet by the head. "Girl, you either pick up that ax and do it quickly or I will find another way that won't be so kind."

I looked at Harriett and she cocked her head to one side, one eye looking at me with confusion. I knew his words were not a threat. He would kill her slowly just to make a point. Even by then, I knew when he meant to teach me a hard life lesson.

I wiped my eyes and reached down with my small shaking hand to lift up the ax.

Daddy smiled at me, beaming with pride. "Atta girl, you know what needs to be done."

I breathed faster, my chest heaved, and I raced to think of any way out of this. I schemed that I would miss her neck and accidentally let her go, but he stretched her thin neck out away from her body with his strong hands. I watched as her little plump chest breathed harder and faster. She tried to shake out of his grip but he was too strong for her, just as he was too strong for me. Holding Harriett steady for me, he waited.

My vision blurred.

Daddy yelled, "Do it *now!*"

I stopped thinking, blocked out all emotion, brought the ax over my head, and cut straight through Harriett's neck in one strong *thunk*. Her body fell to the ground and flopped around. Daddy threw her head to the ground and wiped his hands on his pant leg, leaving finger streaks of blood. I dropped the ax and stepped away.

* * *

From that moment on, I never named our chickens again. Getting close hurt too much. Eventually, I was able to separate this connection and never really thought about it again until tonight. We needed to eat and survive, so chickens, cattle, and deer had to die. But now the man who taught me the importance of cutting out a weak freeloading link is forcing my hand again.

CHAPTER 6

Days turn into months and my daddy's absence no longer surprises me. It's been two weeks since I last saw or heard of him. Since that night when we left him on the ground, covered in his urine and vomit, I don't look for him or bring him back. His staying away was easier actually, and it seems like he must think that too. We aren't sure if he's staying away intentionally or not, but it doesn't matter anymore. I have to focus on my sisters and keep the remnants of our little family together.

Tugging on my boots, I notice the vacant area where his boots used to live.

Distracting myself from the pang of sadness, I get ready for a long day of hunting, fishing, and hopefully some gold panning. I have put off panhandling for months now, burdened with the other more vital tasks that consume my worried mind. Just as I'm saying my goodbyes to Maggie and Lottie, Daddy stumbles into the cabin.

His clothes are caked and darkened from dirt, and his hair is sticking out in all directions in greasy bunches; he can hardly stand. Maggie is holding Lottie who starts to cry from all his commotion. He staggers toward Maggie and Lottie with a crazy look in his eye. All of my hunting senses kick to attention. He never laid a hand on Maggie in the past, so I told myself we had nothing to worry about.

He spits out, "You… You killed your momma, you little witch."

I then notice he is pointing at Lottie. My stomach drops to my feet. He throws the chair across the room and the leg splinters off in pieces. He takes another pounding step at Maggie and Lottie. I attempt to move my body but his eyes snap to mine and I freeze. He keeps looking at me with vacant, lost, and intense eyes, which are lined with silver. He gives me a warning glance, one he had used so many times while we were hunting together. It's a silent order to *stay put.*

I can't move. He then seems to remember Lottie and turns his attention back on her. He stumbles into another chair and braces himself on the kitchen table.

He is taking deep heaving breaths, rasping out the last bit of air he has left. His stance widens, and he stands up.

"If it weren't fer you, your mother would still be alive," he screams.

Lottie screams back at him.

Maggie tries to cover Lottie with her body and turns to back away.

Maggie attempts kindness. "Daddy, why don't you lie down and rest a bit?"

"Annie, don't you tell me what to do," he yells. "It's your fault she's here. You wanted that damn baby. Now, look what she's done."

I saw Maggie's eyes widen; he thinks she is Momma—his Annie.

Maggie starts to move her lips, preparing to say something, but the sound never develops. His body lumbers forward and then time slows to a crawl. I watch stupidly as he charges at my sisters. It isn't until the back of his thick club of a hand connects with the side of Maggie's face that I snap out of my trance.

Maggie falls to the ground, keeping Lottie close to her chest. Without thinking, my hand finds the cast iron pan, the one that heated all our family meals, and I swing it with all my strength. Its weight makes contact with the middle of his back. He cries out in a warbled sound and then tumbles, falling to the ground and clutching his injury.

My whole body is shaking, including both of my hands holding the iron. I raise it above my head, again ready. My fear peaks. I don't know what to do next.

Rising to his knees, my father glares at me with dazed and shining eyes. He closes one of them to focus on me. Good, he is drunk enough to see two of me. At that moment, I am sure I could handle this. I nod my head, telling Maggie to get the hell out of here.

He grabs for her as she runs by with Lottie in her arms but misses and falls to the ground once more. Disgust bubbles in my gut. My shoulders drop and my jaw sets once I see the skirt tails of Maggie's dress exit the front door.

Looking down my nose at him, I bark, "You get out of here, now."

His eyes dart away from mine, with what looks like hurt and betrayal, but I no longer care. He tries to stand but has to crawl over to the sofa to right himself.

He leans on the sofa, and with iciness lacing his words, he taunts me, "What are you gonna do, hit me again?"

"If I have to," I growl without hesitation.

He looks down at the floor as if in defeat, bracing both hands on the spine of the brown leather sofa.

Lowering the pan, relief flits through my body. This subtle movement is all he needs.

He uses the heel of his hand and knocks my chin up. I am thrown off balance and land flat on my back. My head bounces once, and my vision blurs. His balance is thrown by our momentum, causing him to land on me.

Neither of us moves for several moments. We just lie there. The room is twisting around me. His blurred and jerking figure lifts off of me. He stabilizes himself with one hand and punches me hard with the other, making the room spin in the opposite direction.

I blindly swipe his arm with mine and this causes him to fall on his face. Shaking my head several times, my vision clears so I push him over and scramble out from underneath him. I can see in his eyes the explosion of anger burning hotter than I have ever seen it. He might actually kill me.

Move. Move! my head screams to my body.

I raise the pan again, this time over my shoulder, and use a sweeping upward motion to connect with his chin. He falls to the floor and does not get up.

Maggie rushes back into the house with a rifle raised. I am sweating, and my breaths come out of me in ragged grunts. My eyes are wide. She sees Daddy on the ground and then surveys me for any injuries.

"You hurt?"

I shake my head once as tears start to spill over my cheeks. She rushes to me and hugs me. I am drenched in sweat and my heart's still pounding. We allow ourselves a few more moments to calm down.

Pulling away from her, I need space. "He can't be here."

Maggie considers this and nods in agreement. "Let's take him out to the stalls and leave him there. I will clip some money and a note that says to take it, a horse, and to never come back."

Maggie runs to the money jar and fishes out most of our savings. She ties it up in a handkerchief and places it in her apron. I watch her as I sit on the ground. My body continues to shake for a few more seconds, but then my mind catches up and lethal stillness takes over.

I am angry. I let myself think he would never hit Maggie or hurt Lottie. I am angry we are giving him our money, and I am most angry because I can't get myself to move again.

Maggie writes the letter on a piece of paper and grabs a clothespin. I finally drop the pan and am able to rise to my feet. Maggie and I hoist him in the way we had done so many times now. He is deadweight but feels lighter than ever thanks to the renewed conviction and fire that drives us forward.

We drag his body through the dirt to the stables and leave him next to his horse. Maggie clips the note and handkerchief to his shirt. We look at each other and stand a little straighter as we walk back to the cabin. Maggie peels away from me to collect Lottie from the bushes where she hid her. I hold the door open and watch them walk in. I close the door behind me and bolt it shut. We all pile on the sofa. Maggie with Lottie sleeping in her lap and me with the rifle resting across mine. We sit in silence for a long time.

I now only have one goal, and that is to keep my sisters safe from everything. Nothing else matters.

GIVE UP AND GIVE IN

CHAPTER 7

The icy wind seeps deep into my bones. I have not been able to catch food over the last two days and I'm now worried, but I am so tired I almost do not care. After we kicked Daddy out four months ago, the summer months felt manageable and slipped past us dreamily. Maggie and I had prepared by stocking and then re-stocking. We had counted our cans and bought bags and bags of beans and extra dry meat from the Parsons. We rehearsed and replayed all the scenarios that could go wrong.

We didn't account for this type of winter, nor did anyone else. We have never had a winter this bad before. Everyone agrees. Others came to the shop once they all ran out of food earlier than usual. Desperation dissolved from their faces once they saw the shop shelves fully stocked. We made out like bandits with coin and gold, resolving that if we ran out, we would just buy more from the Parson men or I would do some extra hunting. *We are fine,* I reassured myself and Maggie.

However, it is now the dead of deep winter, and supplies and game are scarce. Graham and Daniel have not made it up the mountain for over a month. I have no other choice but to find something out here.

This responsibility is solely on my shoulders. Maggie already offered to help with hunting but neither of us had the patience to endure that lesson. When survival scrapes its hungry claws down my nerves, the nastier side of me is nearly impossible to hide. Teaching Maggie the rudimentary skill of walking quietly ended in a screaming fight. It was a waste of time. Driving her back to the cabin where she was safe was better for us all, I reason with myself.

The looming mountains blanketed in thick white crystals tease my senses. The whitewashed pines lining the ridges are already covered with the same snowy layer; it brings me a sense of wonder and peace. This is an illusion; the beauty of the landscape causes my fears to consume me. The fear of my failure is ever-present, much like the raw skin inside your cheek after you've nipped it with your teeth, never able to leave it alone.

Wearily, I scan the white path in front of me. Foggy thinking as the real reality of our current situation bears down on me and I am not paying attention to where my feet carry me.

You can't do this. You knew you weren't ready. It's all your fault. You should've let him stay. You are the reason they are starving now. Weak, like the girl you are.

Self-loathing comes easily to me with each day, hour, and minute I fail to provide. Times like these Daddy's level of lethal focus used to impress me most. Ever since I was a little girl, I could never understand how he mastered and shoved his needs aside for the hunt. The strength and determination he had exhausted and inspired me on long days.

We would be deep in the mountains together, late at night or early in the morning, and just when I could not bear it anymore, our prey would enter the clearing. He would expertly shoot the beast to the ground.

He would rise from the ground laughing at me and say, "See, if I let you be soft, we would go hungry and die. Toughen up, girl. I do this for your own good."

Focus now. The sharpness and allure of wanting to give up scrapes against my willpower. My mind drifts to another time I almost gave up.

* * *

I was twelve years old, lying in the snow next to Daddy. We'd set our guns and were waiting for the kill. My fingers hurt so bad I believed one of my toes would go black from the wetness and cold that sponged into my boots. A whimper escaped from my pursed lips. The cold numbed my body but also my ability to think straight. Then to add insult to a shitty situation, I had to pee.

Groaning and movements took over my body. Distracted by my primal needs, I never saw the solid heavy elbow flying toward my ribs. I knew when he made contact I would be bruised for weeks. It knocked the wind out of me and I buckled over on my side, gasping for air and wetting myself.

He muttered, "Now you have something to whine about."

I could not breathe.

Just then, the most beautiful doe entered the clearing. My father took a deep breath and cocked the gun, ready to fire, his body set to make a quick and fatal kill.

At the moment just before his finger squeezed the trigger, I unleashed a cry of exaggerated agony.

The doe looked in our direction then swiftly sprinted away.

His anger boiled over at the lost opportunity, so I had to be quick. My size allowed for speed.

My rifle was still attached to me. Tucking my arms, I rolled away as he snatched at the air where I had been. The whiff of his fingertips grazed the rope end of my braided hair.

I still was not able to take deep breaths but I righted myself as best I could and staggered away while holding my already bruising side.

His boots crunched in the snow and mud of the earth, just two strides behind. We had done this before when he was not quite so mad.

He would drive me off so he could find me and tell me all the ways I fucked up by leaving a footprint or being too loud. But that was when I was much younger and now my legs stretched out and I could run lighter and take longer steps. Slowly at first, but when I was able to lengthen my stride to create more room between us, I was sprinting. He was not going to catch me this time.

I could hear him yelling and cursing my name. He was pissed.

One of my trees was just up and around the bend. I had hiding spots all over the mountain for this reason. Alternating between trees and abandoned animal dens kept him guessing and impressed. Sometimes I had to keep running because he figured out that pattern too. I had not escaped up a tree for a while, so this was my option. Also, my ribs were ripping apart with every breath and stride, forcing me to become winded faster than I should've been.

I jumped over the stream, ran past my tree, and kept running. A set of boulders lay just ahead.

Bound, land, pain, breathe.

His heavy boots stomped against the wet forest floor, far enough back that he could no longer see me.

I hit the last rock, fingertips scraping the gritty material, and reached up high for the lowest branch. Launching my body into the air, I pull myself up. Even if he found me, he would not know this maneuver, I mused to myself. Outsmarting him made me smile.

I easily and silently made my way up the tree and got to a place where I could watch him track me. I watched him clear the stream and search the earth in front of him for my footprints. He spotted my path in seconds and kept running, never breaking his pace. I did admire his skills.

He had to slow down because my prints disappeared. He looked around and started to slow his senses down as he had taught me to when tracking animals. He knelt to observe where my boot last touched the ground. Kneeling over and assessing the soil with mastered attention. If an animal darted or jumped to the right there would be more soil to the left.

Even the slightest shift in the soil can give you direction. He'd taught me that too.

So I had practiced jumping straight up and then twisting my body in midair in the direction I wanted to land. He knelt and saw this.

He chuckled and murmured, "Clever girl."

This made me smile too.

I was still mad at him, though, and hoped he would feel stupid after he could not find me. He looked to the boulder and the surrounding trees, which could have been an option for my escape. I was about twenty yards in the opposite direction though. He looked up at the closest surrounding trees but could not spot me since my slender body was easily hidden behind the girth of the tree. He had seen me jump from tree to tree so knew my abilities. He kept looking up and walking away, checking each tree with scrutiny, from different angles, scanning up and down in a repeating pattern.

After surveying every last tree top, his admiration ebbed and anger flowed. He kicked the ground and his breathing became hard and fast.

He yelled at me, "So you don't care if your family goes hungry tonight? I will make sure they know you are the reason."

Guilt from his words dripped like syrup, collecting in my chest, but I knew that was one of his tactics. It had worked on me in the past but would not work on me this time. He was lying anyway. The traps I had set the day before would produce something, and after he gave up on me, I could go collect a squirrel or a rabbit. Smaller this time of year but something to eat. I listened as his temper boiled. He then took off deeper into the forest, and I knew I was safe this time.

I sat up in my tree listening for him and felt extremely pleased with myself. Outsmarting him would make him proud once he calmed down a bit. He never returned for over an hour. My ribs still hurt but I was able to breathe calmly without as much searing pain. I was wet and cold but did not want to come home empty-handed.

I circled out to survey my traps and found the first one empty. I was shocked because this trap usually produced consistently and I had not checked it for two days.

My next closest trap, again there was nothing. This second finding was not too suspicious but when I got to the third one, again no prize, and the trap was destroyed. I knew he had cleared the traps and ruined the third one just to make a point. The old asshole. He would rather have his family starve and make a point. My anger spiked.

I still had my gun, so set out to see if I could kill something to bring home. I set up a spot and hunkered down. I learned that night I was much stronger than I thought I was. Or I realized being stubborn and wanting to prove *my* point gave me renewed energy to stay out in the cold night.

At that moment a small fox entered my view and I took it down, piercing its eye with my bullet. I set to dressing it, so it gave me more time away from the cabin and time for Daddy to calm down.

Maybe I should thank the old shit for this someday, I thought back then.

* * *

I guess today was that day. I proved him wrong then and I will do it now. I can do this. Lethal intensity settles into my bones. I wonder, *Am I really that much different than him?*

CHAPTER 8

With a renewed but fragile sense of purpose, I pull my coat tighter to myself and breathe in the crisp frosty scent. My traps have not been producing lately. Checking my first and closest trap earlier today, I was disappointed that it remained empty. The second trap had more of the same, and the string had not even been triggered. This is not looking good. The third trap does better in the springtime since it is set up by the river. I stop to fill my hunting skin, the icy cold rush of the water stinging my fingertips.

Lasting as long as my fingers can handle it, I fill the skin up nearly halfway and drink deeply. It fills my insides with ripping frigid liquid where I consider if dehydration is worse than this bone-cracking chill one drink elicits from my core. I sip again on the water so as not to shock my body further and then turn my attention to the steep ridge where the last trap is.

Before I move on to my last hope, I settle in and try my hand one more time at hunting. Lying flat on the ground with my rifle propped on a fallen tree, I wait. Then it starts to rain, not snow. I almost start to cry when it turns from a soft drizzle but then dissolves quickly to a downpour. This is my least favorite weather.

As the rain drenches me, my eyes pick up subtle movement. My whole body tenses with anticipation and fear and then begins to tremble thanks to the icy wetness now bypassing my coat and soaking my thick wool tunic. The sensation of internal and external pressure overwhelms my senses. I have to take three deep breaths before I am ready to pull the trigger; my finger quivers, impatient and frantic. I wait too long. The white bobcat hears my breaths and bounds silently away. I fire anyway but miss. I can't take it anymore. I start to scream. Angry tears follow.

All of my doubts stampede back into my mind. Pouring onto my shoulders like the rain drenching my coat.

You can't do this, girl. You are too soft to stay alive on this mountain. You aren't a lady or a hunter so what are you good for?

I can no longer tell if these are my words because he is no longer here, but he is still in my head. Or is it me saying and reinforcing these words because clearly, I am all these things. We are starving, and we've only been six months without him.

You are a failure. You are not good enough.

I did not realize how much he did provide for our family even though I felt I had done all the work, especially in the end. I was wrong. He would always bring extra food home to supplement where I'd lacked. I did not recognize this until we no longer had it, and I couldn't admit to this fact until now when it punches me hard in the gut.

His observation and supplementation were so subtle that I hadn't even noticed he would finally bring something home for the family about the time I ran into trouble. Sure he would remind me of all the ways I failed, with detailed instructions and ways I should've done it better, but at least food was on the table even if my pride took a bruising.

It doesn't matter. He is gone and he is not coming back, and my sisters are hungry. We hadn't heard anything about his whereabouts since the first snowfall. It is raining sheets of ice, and I can't stay any longer. I am not strong enough to endure this, to wait for another chance, in the liquid ice. Even spite is not motivation enough. So I get up and trudge through the snow and ice, the wind howling. With the remaining flicker of energy I have, I set off to my last trap.

The ridge is my last hope but is also the most strenuous to get to, so I consider turning back. All we have are the dregs of grits and molasses. I needed to get back.

Hiking is more difficult now than it should have been. With enough fuel, I could have easily sprinted up this incline, but not now, not today. So a slow steady trudge is all I can muster. It is even too steep for Gunpowder, which is why I chose to work on foot today. Straining my ears for any signs of small animals I could pick off along the way is futile. I hear no sound other than the thud of snow falling off heavy limbs and the persistent pounding of rain.

I'm sweating hard from my boots cracking through the white-crusted surface, dropping each step deep below. Once I reach the ridge, I need my whole body to climb. Now I am fighting the snow and the incline with gloved hands and knees, supporting myself in the upward battle against the mountain, as if both the elements agreed to take me down.

I crest the ridge just as the sun starts to rise over the valley below through the rain. I can see the little town, miles away yet still within view. The sun hits the snow in the valley on the houses and makes the town glow and almost seem welcoming. I know better, though. Yet, I can still appreciate the beauty the winter and sunlight can do to a landscape while also cursing the cozy-looking town and all its inhabitants at the same time.

I am sure they have enough food and are likely wasting it. I had seen their compost, full of vegetables with the little bruised brown tips, which could be easily clipped away, discarded to their pigs as rubbish. It must be nice to live with such luxury.

Straining my neck to the side, I see the trap. Ensnared in it is a small white rabbit, blending in with the snow blanket it lies motionless on. You would think it was sleeping had there not been the smallest amount of crimson pooled beneath it. The spike pierced its heart. I unhook the velvety soft creature. Its limp body flops into the palm of my slender and long fingers. In comparison, this rabbit is dainty like my hands, which like me, are not desirable in these harsh parts. This will have to do though. It's all I have.

I am exhausted and need to eat. I ate the last bit of deer jerky Maggie had insisted I take earlier today. I have to climb back down the ridge and retrace my steps to return home. The march back gives me more time to stew. The woods used to bring me so much peace. Now they just feel like a place where I am alone with my mind, which is not a safe place for me anymore.

Never in my whole life have I wanted to be distracted by my sisters and their needs, even helping around the shop and house, anything to stop the slurry of worry that now haunts the silent moments in my day. Making sleep impossible, racing worries fought me the whole night and now during the day.

When I see the cabin I can't help but sigh a puff of relief. The constant smoke coming out of the chimney is a sign that they are well and warm.

CHAPTER 9

I open the door and Maggie looks up at me, her furrowed brows relax, and her face lights up. I knock my boots on the side of the doorframe and shake off as much of the snow and moisture as I can. She rushes over to me and helps me peel off my sopping fur coat and the many layers, which make me look bigger than I am. They've kept me as warm and dry as possible.

Maggie has found a way to line my coats and boots with the outermost layer of the animal hide and then uses animal wax to treat the coat to keep the water out from reasonable elements. This winter is anything but reasonable to us. She does it to our shoes as well. She created this technique, which makes her coats and clothing much more valuable in our parts.

Her clothes are coveted. We have families come up in the summertime to place an order to have them before winter for Christmas gifts. She keeps perfecting this and people keep coming. We have repeat customers who can afford it. She uses the townsfolk and the wealthy in her own way to keep perfecting her craft. For me, they are just a way of life now, and I thank her every day for her attention to comfort and utility. Not to mention she makes them look good. I catch myself reaching out all the time to touch the clothing to better appreciate her skill whenever a customer comes to take their prize away.

Maggie is putting the pot on the stove to boil water while Lottie sits on the floor next to the fire playing with her doll. The warmth of the fire is beckoning me to come closer. I hurry to close the thick wooden door to keep the heat in. My muscles relax instantly. I pull out the pathetic velvety rabbit and hand it to Maggie.

She accepts it with grace and exclaims, "Oh, thank God, El. I knew you could do it."

I roll my eyes at the optimism yet also have an inner sense of pride in the way she always shows appreciation for my time in the woods. Even though we fight and are both stubborn as mules, we still appreciate the other's roles and skills. No matter if I bring home a bear or a squirrel, she finds joy in it. I find value in the bounty as well, and the size correlates to my worth. Right now I am not worth much.

I peel off my boots and sit on the floor with Lottie, who crawls over and lifts her arms to me. She wants up. Her fat arms and legs wrap around my midsection, and I squeeze her in, inhaling her soft clean scent. I play with her downy light brown curls at the nape of her neck and squeeze her tightly. She starts to wiggle and wants back down and for me to play dolls with her. She gets the pretty doll with the dress and always gives me the grimy tin toy soldier to play with. *Fitting.* I smile.

I play along with her as Maggie starts to skin the rabbit and organize all the contents.

Maggie looks at me and says, "Ellie, you look so tired."

I say, "I am always tired." I would sleep the whole next day if I could. I know I can't, so I push it out of my mind.

Maggie urges, "You should bathe and go to bed. When you wake up, I will have the rabbit stew ready. I found a jar of potatoes I can add to it. In the meantime, here are some coffee and grits. I want you to eat that now before your bath."

I do as I am told because arguing with Maggie would take too much energy. So I eat most of my grits but leave a bit so Maggie has to give the rest to Lottie. Maggie knows this trick but apparently also decides this fight is not worth it either. The rain on the roof slows. Maybe the Parson men will be able to make the trip up the mountain to trade in the next few days.

Leaving the main room, I peel the rest of my sopping clothes off in the washroom. Maggie's pot of water starts to boil. I smile because she knew I would be home and had the fire under the tub lit and ready. The metal tub is filled so it just needs topping off. She dumps the boiling water into the tub, and the steam rises off the surface, wispy fingers curling and beckoning me to come closer. The room is dark with the tub and fire directly in the center. I can see my haggard reflection in a large vanity and wash basin. Maggie leaves without a word as I climb in.

I sit with my legs bent into my body as I clean myself with Maggie's honey-smelling soap. I wash everywhere, feeling the curvature of my womanly body develop and change with each year. My full breasts and thighs have widened as if my body is preparing for something else when all I wish for it to do is remain lean and muscular. My curves are now getting in the way when I run and jump.

I look down at my winter pale skin and clean the half-moon-shaped grime from under my nails. The heat from the water and flames stings my skin as the cold slowly seeps from my bones. I hear the crackle under the tub and settle in, even the aroma of the smoke calms me with its musky pine notes. I have now cleaned my body and can stretch my legs out of the tub. I tilt my head back to relax and exhale, allowing my muscles to finally loosen. I close my eyes.

I used to relax my neck over the edge of the tub this way. Momma would come in at this point so she could help me brush out my wavy brunette hair. She used the brush to lightly comb out the tangles as she talked to me softly. She said it was because I didn't brush it out right, yet we both knew we used it as an excuse to be alone together. It was our time. She never expected me to respond or talk unless I wanted to.

Her hand followed the brush stroke coaxing me to relax. "You are a good girl. You are so smart and do so much for this family. Now relax." She used to kiss me on the temple and quietly leave the room to give me space.

The door creaks, and I wake up. I'd dozed off. Years have passed since my mother brushed my hair. I slit open my eyes to adjust to the light streaming into the room. I was dreaming of my mother.

The thudding of knees and hands makes its way across the wooden floor to me. Lottie's grunts and struggle make me lightly chuckle as she pulls her little body up the step. Tiny fingers slide over the lip of the tub. Her face barely clears the height and I see big blue eyes that sparkle. I lower my head so we are eye to eye. I can see her little smile touch her eyes, and I raise my lips over the tub's edge and give her little nose a big wet kiss. She screams and laughs. Maggie runs in and swoops her up into her arms.

"Lottie, you little fox." Maggie hadn't noticed Lottie sneak away. Lottie was laughing and pouting in Maggie's arms as she whisked our little sister out of the room.

I decide it's time to get out of the tub and get dressed. As I lift my sore body from the tub, I feel the chill of the rest of the house hit my pale wet skin. I quickly dry myself and dress in the thick pants and tunic my sister made for me during the winter months. Everything fits so perfectly. Leaving the bathroom, I smell of honey and have clean skin. With my mother's silver brush in hand, I pad back into the living room and start to brush my own hair.

Maggie is still working on the rabbit and cleaning it. I lie on the brown full leather sofa and lounge there. I am most at ease now during these moments. Knowing my sisters are safe, fed, and warm is the only time I can truly relax. Maggie hands me a warm cup of coffee, and I inhale the rich smoky fragrance. I slowly sip and listen to the sounds around me. The rain is still coming down. We desperately need the Parsons to make it up to us and soon; maybe the rain will clear the snow away enough.

Maggie finally sits down next to me on the sofa, and I lift the blanket for her to crawl under. We sip coffee together and sit in silence.

"Maggie, I didn't realize how much he had helped us out. I mean, I know it wasn't much in the end but I don't know if I can do this alone."

"You are not alone. You have us. And with fewer mouths to feed, we can ration the food better with this next haul that will come any day."

I look at her out of the corner of my eye and then look down at my coffee. "But what if they can't get up to us?"

Maggie looks at me and then at the fireplace. With determination and trust, she simply says, "Then your traps will keep us alive."

Bitterly I sigh out, "Hardly."

Maggie reaches over and grabs my hand as our eyes meet. Maggie has the kindest softest blue eyes, which calm my nerves at this moment. "Hardly is better than not at all."

I lay my head against her shoulder and allow myself to rest. I put my cup down and close my eyes.

I sleep for a long time before the smell of the hearty stew wakes me up. Maggie must've gotten up to continue her work on the rabbit. Curled up in my arms are Lottie and her little doll. I lie there a bit longer just soaking up the heat and comfort her little body emits.

Forcing my muscles to move, I ease Lottie onto the sofa. She is sucking her thumb, a habit we needed to break, eventually. Walking over to the counter, I inhale the smell of the roasted meat, starchy potatoes, and the spicy mix of salt, pepper, and nutmeg.

Maggie hums, notes my presence, and without a word, scoops the thickened stew into a wooden bowl and hands it to me. Then, she scoops one for herself. We sit at the table and savor in silence, simply happy in each other's presence.

I look around at all the empty chairs that now surround our table. The table was built for six people but only two remain. Now it seems so empty.

My mind wanders back to those times of warmth and laughter that could fill this room. My father and I would have caught the meat, my sister and mother would have baked the bread and harvested the garden, and the table would be full of all of our contributions. The satisfaction enhanced the happiness, safety, and simply being together. We were a happy family in those moments. I hold those moments most dear.

Maggie and I look at each other and realize we were both somewhere else and likely within the same memories. We both lightly smile.

She says, "So the Parsons are likely coming in the next few days. Will you stick close to home to see them?"

Confidently I respond, "Yes, I will. We must be much more tactful this time around."

Maggie looks at me and says, "Yes, it is the *only* reason why you want to be here when they make the trip to see us."

I look at her straight in the eyes. "Yes, *it is* the *only* reason. We must be smarter about this if we want to survive up here through the rest of this wretched winter."

Maggie continues to look at me with coy insinuation. "So seeing them doesn't mean *anything* more than business to you?"

"What are you trying to say?"

Maggie shrugs and fans herself. "They aren't hard on the eyes."

"Maggie!"

"What? You can't deny it, El. They are handsome men."

I start to think about it, and of course, my body starts to respond. Just the image of Graham makes me a little warmer to my core. I have not admitted it to anyone else but my mind does drift to Graham often when I am out in the woods alone. And truth be told, my womanly body has betrayed me a few times when my primal needs took over. I have used the image of a certain dark-haired, blue-eyed man a few times to satiate my needs when I am alone in the woods.

My cheeks heat up and blush. I fear Maggie notices my daydreaming so I look down at my stew.

"Maggie, just eat your food," I say to end the conversation.

She smiles into her stew, and I roll my eyes.

I change the subject. "What are you working on now?"

She looks at me with fire in her eyes and a broad smile swipes up. "Do you want to see it?"

Before I even answer, she is up and running into the next room. I savor the last few bites of my stew, enjoying how it fills and warms me from within. She is rummaging around in the next room and then runs out clad in a white fur coat. She is all smiles, puffed up with pride in the way she only ever is when she is working on her craft. Her confidence is brightest in these moments.

I take in the coat as it hugs her delicate frame. It is striking, but it is cropped and extenuates her thin waist, making her look very feminine.

"Where did the other half of the coat go?" I tease.

She rolls her eyes and says, "Not everything has to be made for utility."

I beg to differ. I just do not understand wearing anything unless it is to protect or make my jobs easier.

She sighs with exacerbation and loses a little of her confidence. I put my spoon down and try to see what she is seeing.

"All right, Maggie, let me take a closer look." I walk to her, and she starts explaining.

"So picture this. One of the merchants' wives wears it to town around Christmas time. She is dressed in a warm dress with this coat layered over its top. It sits just here." She points to her slender waist, cinched in. "Also, look at the bone-toggle fastens I carved out of pieces of the fox's leg. They are in a triangular shape so they will stay together and can be admired if someone chooses to get closer."

The toggles are textured with wavy lines carved in them, tiny little grooves using the grain of the natural bone and adding little connections to create the design. The toggle is secured by tiny leather loops.

She shrugs out of the coat and then hands it to me. Even the stitching on the inside is stunning. The seam is fashioned in a zig-zagging pattern to strengthen the line and decorate the piece as well.

Maggie holds it out for me to step into. I look at her and shake my head. There is no reason for me to put this on. It will look ridiculous on me. She rolls her eyes again.

"It's not for you. It's for me. I just want to see how it looks on another woman."

I hardly count as that but I appease her. Pulling on the coat, it is tighter than I am used to. My shoulders are slightly wider than hers thanks to the toned muscle beneath. The coat does show off my silhouette. Maggie grabs my arm and pulls me to the mirror. There I see myself and realize I actually look pretty. Not delicate but womanly and elegant. Striking even.

I turn my body to look at the side and over my shoulder. It really is a pretty coat but still, I just don't see who would buy something like this. I have to admit it is a work of art. She comes up next to me and unbuttons the bottom two toggles.

"See, you can also wear it as a shawl in warmer weather and inside," says Maggie.

"Mags, it is beautiful," I admit earnestly

She beams at me and then exclaims, "Oh, the earmuffs!"

She runs into her sewing room and comes out with her half-complete project. One-half of the earmuff is fashioned with the hide of the white rabbit I caught last week. It is stitched to a singular fox rib to fit over a small head. She thrusts it over my head and one of my ears is muffled. Now I look ridiculous. I yank it off and throw it at her. Carefully taking the coat off, I hand it to her as well. She pouts but smiles, looking down at her pieces with pride.

Sorrow sags my brow as I realize Maggie is not meant for this hard life. She should be married to a wealthy man and live in comfort, not this. She is stuck here, and it caves in my chest, knowing this life was thrust upon her with no way out. Now with our little sister Lottie, the chances of her finding a suitor are even grimmer.

So she's left with just me to survive the only way we know how, together. It is the only way.

CHAPTER 10

Fuck this weather. It is the heavy hammer nailing our coffin lid shut. At first, it let up and the rain washed away the snow and ice, but now the road is covered again with several feet of snow. No way would the Parsons' wagon make it up to us. Another month passes with no sign of help.

"Ellie, we have to *do* something." Maggie could no longer keep the worry out of her eyes or voice.

"Nothing is out there," I admit finally, defeated.

"What about asking the others for help?" Maggie suggests.

"I already have. No one has anything to trade or give us." Reality dropped an iron in my gut after I asked around all this week. Asking for help like this has drained all the remaining pride I have.

Many neighbors have abandoned their cabins, and the ones who stayed are just as hard up as we are. Everyone expected us to have the supplies, and since we're out, we are all doomed. Not only did I fail my sisters but also my mother's legacy and the community that counted on us.

Maggie's jaw is set as she says, "Then you have to go. You have to make the trip to town and bring us back supplies."

"No, I will not leave you. That is not an option." My jaw sets harder in response. I could not—no, *would* not—entertain this idea.

"What other choice do we have? This is our choice." Her worried face side-eyes Lottie as she stirs in her sleep.

We both pause, suspending our discussion. Relief washes over us when our baby sister doesn't fully wake. Sleep at least takes the pangs of hunger away. We do not want to wake her from the escape.

Lowering my voice, I continue, "Leaving you here by yourself? Word would get out fast. Desperate men do desperate things." I try not to imagine what those things would be. Just the other day, Maggie and I fought off a starving drifter. We were both home that time but had I been out hunting, I cringe at the possibility.

"We are starving to death," Maggie whispers, struggling to keep her voice calm and steady.

We've each been holding it together for the sake of the other but I can feel the restraint starting to buckle.

"We have the horses. I could shoot one of them and then we would be fed for weeks." I can't believe I just said those words. Betraying me further, the growl in my stomach twists and riles as if in agreement. We both hear it.

"We can't do that. They are our only way off this God-forsaken mountain. If it comes down to it, we need them to escape."

I know she is right but I persist. "I will not leave you, Maggie."

"Then we will die." Her fear and desperation finally win out, and her voice rises in emphasis.

Lottie wakes up from her voice and starts to whimper, which quickly dissolves into a screaming fit.

Well, she is up now, so all bets are off.

"*You* will die, or worse be raped, and then left to die if I leave. I can't do that." I'm shaking now with rage and fear at our dire situation.

"I have guns. I know how to use them, Ellie. You have to go."

Lottie's shrieks pierce my ears. Her octave indicates her hunger and pain. I can't take the sound.

If I stay, we wither and waste. But if I go, there is no telling who will take advantage of their exposure. Lottie is too little and the weather is too harsh to take her with us.

I can't make this decision. The emptiness in my belly and the lack of sleep haunt me and cloud my judgment.

Stomping away to finally pick up Lottie, Maggie tries to console our baby sister. We both know no amount of rocking or shushing will work.

Another iron is added to the stack weighing down my insides. We both know what I have to do.

Defiantly, I pack my bags. Lottie's incessant screaming rakes down my last nerves and strength. Guilt and anger pound at me like a rotting tooth that needs to be yanked out.

Getting ready takes almost no time at all since we don't have anything to eat. All I need is my coat and my horse.

"Maggie, you do not open this door for anyone. You hear me, girl?" Biting my warning out at her, my tone sounds like someone else we both knew.

"Don't you bark orders at me. You are starting to sound just like him." She knows this will wound me.

"At least he taught me some sense. All Momma taught you was to be a good little girl—and look where that got her. You will end up in the grave the same way she did." I sling this weapon back at her.

"You go on thinking that and see where it gets you. You'll be alone and miserable like him," Maggie screams and turns her back on me.

Snatching my rifle and the wooden door handle, I pause for only a moment. I consider that this might be the last time I see my sisters. A better person could shelf this fight and offer a kinder goodbye, but I am not a better person.

"Just don't be stupid or let that sappy heart of yours get you killed," I say as I slam the door behind me. This door and I work well together to have the last word.

Stomping to the stables, I prepare to leave. I'm already fighting the wind and the sideways rain. Looking at the blizzarding road ahead makes me doubt I will ever make it back—let alone to town in one piece. The pit in my stomach drops out and apathy sets in. There is no use. They are as good as dead and so am I.

CHAPTER 11

White flakes lash my face. Little pelting daggers sting the only exposed skin surrounding my eyes. The blizzarding storm is blinding. Only layers of white and the weight of an object provide contrast. Looking down and turning away, I brace myself against the howling wind and snow. Gunpowder trudges on, also lowering his long nose to power through the weather.

Progress is slow and questionable. Each step is combated by deep snowy drifts and wind knocking us with solid punches from every angle. I pull up my black bear skin coat collar and push down my large-brimmed black hat to shut out as much of the cold and reality as I can.

Tightening the reins over my double leather-gloved hand, I tie a knot lassoing myself to my horse. This tether and relying on Gunpowder knowing the way are the only form of a compass I have. Even though Gunpowder is as steady as he can be, I am also riding the storm that nearly bucks me off his back several times. Between the elements and my faintness, my world is spinning literally and figuratively.

My mother's legacy was our shop. She pulled us out of poverty, but was it worth it? Relying on the land and the Parson men put us here. I hated depending on them. And now without them, we couldn't make it. Defeat and shame settle low in my belly, coiled and tight.

I can no longer tell what is sky or earth. The whistling of the wind blocks out any other sounds. I can't stand reality any longer. Distracting myself from the past, I wonder, how did we get here?

* * *

Ten years ago, Momma finally decided to set up our shop. When she first mentioned it to Daddy, he laughed and said no one would come. Word got out that we had supplies, so mountaineers, gold miners, and bootleggers alike stopped by just to see what we had. Most of these men did not have women in their lives, so they would bask in the feminine attention Momma provided.

She packed products small and ready-made with items that made their lives easier. Travel-sized coffee tins, jerky portioned out large enough to satisfy a man's hunger, and cookies that were sturdy but buttery soft once you dunked them in coffee were the most popular. After everyone knew we were open for business, we never had a day or even night when someone wouldn't visit us.

The next closest place to purchase supplies was in town. Not only would they have to buy larger amounts and then portion them out themselves, but going to town was a burden. The mountain folk did not mingle with the townies, which was about the only thing we and the townies agreed upon.

Neighbors would tell Momma, "Those townies are too tightly strung" and would thank my family for saving them the trip. Shootouts, broken glass, and fights followed almost every time these worlds collided.

At first, Momma stocked baked goods, candles, meat, jerky, and clothing she made from the animals Daddy killed. People bought our supplies faster than she could keep the shelves stocked. Eventually, they asked for supplies we couldn't make or find in the woods such as rope, salt, dried goods, and such. More and more people would ask for these supplies, and Momma or Maggie had to tell them the closest place was back in town. Grumbling, they left but thanked us anyway.

Back then, we were too little to be much help. Maggie and I sat at the dinner table and practiced our letters as Momma corrected our mistakes on the morning the deal was made. The biggest four-horse-drawn wagon I had ever seen lumbered up the drive. I had only seen this wagon once before parked out in front of the Parson's Mercantile.

Mr. Parson was the owner of the only one-stop-shop in town. Everyone got their supplies there, and we were no different, but this was the first we ever saw them out here. Word had it he was establishing trading routes between the neighboring towns and becoming the man to deal with, but he mainly kept the locals stocked.

Everyone knew and liked him. Mr. Parson had even given Maggie and me some candy for free when my parents were not looking the last time we visited town. In fact, he and his son were the only townies who didn't sneer at us or lift their upper lips in disgust as we passed by. The sweetness of the candy didn't make up for the others, though. When my family visited last, the mothers wouldn't let their darling babies play with us and quickly ushered them away as if we were feral animals. It was the last time I visited town.

Eventually, Daddy stopped taking all of us and instead would go with other mountain men, claiming strength in numbers. He would return bloody and drunk.

Momma peered out the window and hollered for Daddy. He was out back working on the barn. The look on my daddy's face even lifted in surprise at our unexpected visitors. Dusting off his pants and stomping his feet, he motioned for my momma to meet him outside. Maggie and I followed.

Bobbing up the uneven road, next to Mr. Parson, was his son, Graham. I had seen him once before but I had never talked to him. Graham held the leather reins instead of his father, which was odd. Graham couldn't have been much older than me at the age of ten. It clearly was not his first time, either. The fluid ease and confidence in his motions were impressive.

Continuing up the road, their dark, almost black, heads of hair were covered in matching warm brown leather cowboy hats. Graham was a miniature version of his father. Mr. Parson was handsome, or so Maggie said, but I didn't pay any mind to those things. As they drew closer, I noticed both had blue eyes. Daniel's were lighter, a cool blue, but Graham's were darker like the color of a stormy sky. Rolling up to meet my parents, they stopped a few yards away.

"Hello, I am Daniel Parson and this is my son Graham Parson." Daniel raised both his hands lightly in the air.

Daddy had one arm possessively around my momma's shoulders and the other on his pistol.

Daddy nodded. "I know who you are. What brings you up here?"

"Well, I heard about your shop, and I figured we needed to pay a visit to the new business owners," Daniel said earnestly.

"I brought a gift I wanted to give the missus." Daniel reached behind him, and my father tightened the grip on his gun.

Daniel spun around and had a basket of flowers, dried goods, and bottles with ribbons tied to them. Even I could admit it looked pretty.

Daddy whistled. "That sure looks like a fancy basket, Annie."

Momma nodded and waited for Daddy to give her more direction.

Daddy dropped his arm from around my mother's slender shoulders and walked up to the wagon. Daniel and Graham were sitting up high and looked down at Daddy as he approached. Tension laced the air, and Daniel instinctively positioned his body in front of Graham. Scanning the wagon, I found Graham's eyes were on me. His dark blue eyes bored straight at me. He kept looking longer than what was polite. Momma always said not to stare but I felt a stand-off between Daddy and Daniel. I wanted to glare at Graham to show that I wouldn't back down, either.

Graham's lips crack into a full-faced smile. It was the first time I ever saw Graham's smile. It took up half of his face; the lightness of it threw me off. Jutting my chin out and widening my eyes, I stood my ground. He just continued to stare and smirk, so I stared right back. Maggie elbowed me in the side hard enough to break my concentration, and I glared at her for it. Focusing back on the adults, I resolved to ignore this arrogant boy. His daddy was probably no better.

Daniel offered Daddy his hand in good nature and they shook firmly. Both muscled tanned arms squeezed tightly. I knew when two male bucks were facing off. There was snorting, puffing up, and stamping of hooves. Grown men I guess weren't much different, just less dramatic. Daniel jumped off the wagon, and Graham followed him down. Daddy remained close to Daniel in his space, no indication the city slicker would intimidate him. Daniel handed Daddy the basket, and I sensed a little of the tension uncoil now that his hands were full. Whenever he was tense, I was tense.

Daddy carried over the pretty basket for Momma to inspect, Daniel and Graham flanking just behind. I sneaked a peek over at Graham, my annoyance bubbling back up. He was looking at me again! What was his problem? Lifting my chin higher in the air, I made a point to snub him and walked to the cabin next to Maggie.

"Won't you come in and have some tea with us?" Momma offered politely.

"Thank you, ma'am." Daniel removed his hat and ushered Graham forward. Graham looked back at me again, and I stuck my tongue out at him. Graham giggled, and Maggie rolled her eyes. I did enjoy irritating my sister when I could, so I smiled too.

Daniel surveyed the shop and our cabin. "William, your craftsmanship is stunning. Did you build all this?" Daniel ran his hand along the smooth edges of the shelves and admired them.

Daddy answered curtly, "Of course. Every man should know how to work wood."

Daniel shook his head. "Indeed. Unfortunately, craftsmanship is not my strong suit. I tend to do better in the bartering and trading world."

Daddy sneered. "Wheeling and dealing, huh?"

Daniel shrugged. "I reckon I can use my gift for gab and suppling those who *are* more capable than me to live their lives easier. I find purpose in keeping people stocked and prepared, to support the life they want to live." He looked over at Graham before continuing. "And now it's just me and Graham, I want to leave him with something to grow and develop over time if he wants to."

Momma was busy boiling water and setting out cookies to eat. She had a coy smile on her lips and nodded her head at Daniel's words in what I assumed was solidarity.

Daddy and Daniel finally sat down at the table. Maggie and I cleared our books and sat in the remaining chairs in silence. Graham was sitting in the chair across from me. His feet did not touch the wooden floor as he kicked his feet back and forth. This made me smile when I noticed I was doing the same thing. Steeling back up, I still was not sure how we felt about the Parsons, so made sure I didn't commit to liking Graham yet. I was waiting for Daddy's verdict.

My mother brought over the teacups, and Maggie got up to help her without any prompting. She placed spoons next to each person and a little plate. Momma insisted on some finery, and this was one of them. These ones had little blue forget-me-nots painted on them and were my favorite. I hoped these townies would be careful with them.

Daddy did not even pretend to drink the tea and lightly pushed the teapot away. He reached into his breast pocket and poured the brown liquor into the pretty tea cup. At least the brown color looked like he was drinking tea too.

He leaned back in his chair and again wrapped his arm around my mother possessively. She was his.

"Why are you really here?" Daddy asked bluntly.

Daniel set his teacup down before he began to talk, just the way Momma had taught us to do in our manners lessons. Maggie always remembered to do this but I often forgot. I talked with my mouth full and put my elbows on the table too. I was an embarrassment, Maggie always said.

"As I said, I wanted to meet you. Word has it you are lifesavers out here suppling the mountain folk, and I wanted to see how I could support your business." He looked at Daddy first and then at Momma.

"Ha! I wouldn't call this much of a business. Annie got bored out here in the wild and needed to find a way to pass the time. I built her this big house to fill it with boys. No luck so far." Leaning over, he gave Momma a big wet kiss on the cheek. I couldn't help but notice Momma's wounded half blink followed by a polite smile.

Daniel did not smile at this, which I appreciated. "I am thankful every day I have Graham but I sure would have treasured a baby girl too. Something to remember about my beautiful wife Beatrice. She passed away last year."

Daddy huffed out a breath and drained the contents of the teacup down his throat.

Momma sipped her tea and then set it down. "We are sorry for your loss. Regarding our shop, we are doing quite well. I sure would like to offer more nonperishables and other supplies that we can't produce ourselves. There is demand for those items. The half-day journey back to town makes the locals uncomfortable. I wish we had a way to get those supplies here." Momma's eyes had a knowing sparkle in them.

Daniel and my momma seemed to know something I didn't. I kept a close eye on Daddy to see if he was in on it.

"Say, Daniel, what if you and I strike up a deal? You bring us the most common goods so we can make a profit and you don't have to deal with us as often," Daddy suggested.

Momma looked at Daddy. "Now that is an idea, William. Mr. Parson, what do you think about that?" She locked eyes with Daniel. Their blue eyes met and communicated something silently, it seemed.

"Please call me Daniel. Graham and I could come up here once a month at first to see how supplies distribute, and then once it becomes more steady more often—if that suits you all?" Daniel looked at Daddy directly with this question.

"Yeah, yeah, sounds fine. Now let's talk money."

"With my other suppliers, I offer an agreement of ten percent of the profit," Daniel said confidently.

"I won't take anything less than twenty. You townies have to deal with the roughnecks on occasion. We have to deal with them daily. Twenty will cover the risk to my wife and baby girls since they are the ones who have to deal with it."

Daniel smiled. "Done."

Momma's eyes widened.

Daddy whooped out a laugh. He reached his hand across the table and shook Daniel's hand. It was a deal.

"Let's celebrate our new business partner. Annie, get the Apple Pie Moonshine for our guests."

Momma obliged.

As she put out the bottle, I could see the pulp from the apple settled on the bottom. Momma shook it hard a few times to mix it together and then poured each of the adults two fingers worth into her nice tea cups. I didn't like that stuff touching Momma's nice cups. Picking up the cups, they clinked them together and drained them down.

Daniel coughed, and Daddy laughed at him. Picking up the mason jar this time, Daddy poured the sweet liquid into the cups, bringing the level just below the lip. He eyed Daniel, and they drank it down again. My momma sipped this one out.

"You kids go play outside while we figure out the rest of this," Momma said, knowing how Daddy got on the 'shine especially when competition was involved.

Maggie objected, "Can I go read my book instead?"

Momma stroked Maggie's hair and nodded once.

"Then can I show Graham my gun?" I begged, using the light energy in the room to get my way.

"Sure, Ellie. Show that city boy how a real country girl can shoot," Daddy said, pouring another drink for himself and Daniel.

"Ellie, you be careful," Momma warned.

"I know," I whined and ran into our room to grab my rifle.

Graham was out of his chair waiting for me. My heart fluttered a bit knowing we'd be alone.

Daniel looked at Graham, walked over, and kissed him on the head. "Be careful and don't get too far away—hollerin' distance at least okay?"

"Okay, Dad," Graham said.

"Don't worry. Ellie will protect him," Daddy taunted.

"I don't need protection," Graham said defensively.

I grabbed his hand and pulled him out of the cabin before anyone could respond. I didn't want my parents' good mood ruined by this snobby boy. We ran out into the warm spring day.

* * *

Crunching in the snow snaps me back to this winter day and my current situation. Gunpowder and I have not yet hit the halfway mark, meaning the half-day trip will take all day and likely into the night.

Looking up, I notice three dark figures in the distance atop horses. Shit, I do not have the energy to ward off anyone. I sit up and absorb the blast of wind as it pushes into my chest, one hand on my pistol, the other positioning my rifle across my lap for easy access.

Who the hell would be out in this mess unless they were lost? Praying the blizzard has whipped them as hard as it's punishing me, I'm hopeful their energy is low, too.

"You all better turn back around where you came from. It just gets worse from here," I warn.

The three figures are covered from head to toe with furs, boots, and gloves. I scan all three pairs of hands, noting how close they are to their pistols.

"Mister, do you live up here?" one of the gruff men asks.

They can't tell I am a woman. Thank God for that.

"I do, and I know there is nothing and no one back there, so you best turn around and get." I drop my voice for emphasis.

"Have you stopped by the shop they have out there?" the other asked pointedly.

"I have, and they don't have anything left. That family is gone," I lie.

"Gone, what do you mean?"

"I'm not sure. If they were smart enough, they would have left before this snow flew. I haven't seen them for weeks." I'm scanning their movements to see if they bought it.

I watch as they look at each other and exchange some words.

"You all look well-stocked. Where are you headed in this storm?" I ask warily. Maybe I can buy some of their supplies *and* turn them around.

"Well, we are the suppliers who stock these parts. We reckon folks are struggling out here. We have been trying to get our wagon up here for weeks but the weather hasn't let up."

I whip off my hat and let my hair fall. It's them. We are saved.

"Ellie, is that you?" The rider in the front lifts his hand to shield his eyes and tries to focus. His familiar voice is music on the wind.

Tears sting my eyes as the recognition travels across his face.

Graham takes off, spurring his horse to move faster. My body slumps, and I let my rifle fall to the ground. Relief washes over me. Graham dismounts his horse and is at my side like a dream.

His arms reach up for me, and I accept his offer. Lowering my body down, I let him support my weight.

Graham's frantic eyes are rapidly scanning me for any injury. His hands are on my too-thin ribs. His face tells me everything. I see a mix of relief and sadness flit across his chiseled features.

"Do you have any water?" I say through chapped lips.

He doesn't say anything just deftly finds his waterskin and hands it over to me. I drink greedily as I eye the six full water satchels on the horses.

"Ellie, are you okay?" His eyes search for any clues of trauma.

"I am now." Relief seeps from my response. More proof that I couldn't do it on my own.

"Ellie, what did you mean your family is gone?" Daniel was there now, fear and desperation in his eyes.

"Maggie and Lottie are still there. They are starving so I had to leave," I reply without looking him in the eyes.

"But they are alive?" Daniel pushes with more urgency than I would expect.

"Yes, they were alive the last time I saw them. But everyone is struggling out there. The only thing left is liquor. People have been coming by to see if we have anything left. We've had to ward them off."

Daniel doesn't respond and just takes off in a full-on gallop. Tommy, their hired adolescent help and the third figure, is flanking him with more supplies, I realize.

My attention snaps back to Graham.

"Ellie, you are skin and bones." He pulls me into his warm body, rubbing my arms to create friction.

Shivering into him, I loosen a breath and shudder. "You came."

"I was trying to make it to you for weeks. Finally, I couldn't wait any longer. We packed the horses as much as we could and took off yesterday."

The word *yesterday* reverberates across my mind and the reality that I would not have made it to tomorrow sets in. I am too defeated to feel anything. Numbness is all I have left.

Graham reads my expression and hugs me tighter. He climbs onto his horse and offers his gloved hand out to me. I mount his horse with him and wrap my arms around his waist. Graham pulls Gunpowder to us, and we take off at a quick pace. His hand rests on both of my clasped gloved hands, and he rubs them gently. I lean my head into his thick coat and drift off to the familiar scent of pine oil and my friend.

CHAPTER 12

Graham's firm body stirs as he sits up a little taller. I notice his horse has stopped, and this wakes me up gently. The full weight of my body is pressing into his broad warm back. Lifting my head, I try to orient myself. We are back at the cabin and close to the stalls. My hands are sweaty from our fingers being intertwined. My cheeks heat up; I release from him and position myself to dismount his horse.

Did I grab his hand or did he grab mine? I'm begging to God that he grabbed mine. As we grew up, moments like these became something I craved but never allowed myself to indulge in. Closeness, knees touching, teasing, and light pushes were all part of our bantering play but never for longer than the briefest of brushes.

He halts us at the stalls so I dislodge myself from his body and slide to the crusty ground. I tend to Gunpowder and Graham's horse as an excuse to keep my now-empty hands busy.

"Let me do that, Ellie." Graham grabs for the reins.

"No, I've got it," I say, refusing to look him in the eyes.

Graham steps directly in my way, squaring off in front of me and forcing my gaze to meet his.

"Ellie, no. You need to go inside and get some food," he says with authority.

"I will help you out here and then we will go in together." I will not let him take care of our horses and my family by himself. I am not a freeloader. The fact that I needed help is shameful enough.

Our eyes level with the threat of an argument silently communicated.

"Fine," he agrees.

We tend to the horses, feeding and watering them, before securing them under their blankets. Packing some of the supplies in, we meet Maggie, Daniel, and Tommy in the cabin.

Maggie is already playing hostess while Tommy holds and plays with Lottie. Daniel stocks the shelves, and I notice his brows are no longer stitched together. He appears relaxed, his shoulders down and in action.

I help Graham unload the packs and separate supplies into groups. A well-oiled operation, Graham and Daniel organize items on the shelves in the way Momma had always done. I chalk it up to them being seasoned storefront owners but can't shake the respect and attention to detail. They've always shown this level of attention to us.

Finishing up rather quickly, Maggie shoves a steaming hot beverage into my hands. It wafts a scent of coffee and whiskey. Sipping it through my lips, the sweetness of honey is also welcome. We had not said a direct word to each other yet. Neither of us is ready to apologize.

Maggie made enough coffee for all and we sit around the fire in chairs and on the sofa once the chores are done. Daniel and Tommy had beaten Graham and me to the cabin by a good half hour. Daniel had brought pre-marinated and ready-to-cook beef, and Maggie had already started to roast it. The fat meaty aroma of beef makes my mouth water.

Cookies, nuts, bread, jerky, and dried fruit are out now. Maggie, Lottie, and I try to restrain ourselves but Daniel and Graham take turns refilling the little dishes Maggie uses to present these items without permission or hesitation.

Aromas of coffee, cooking meat, potatoes, onions, and carrots fill the cabin, taking over the tension with a sense of ease from all. Even my shoulders seem to drop an inch as we sit and finally recover from our ride. The room goes silent.

Thank goodness Maggie, ever the hostess, speaks up. "We are so thankful for you all. I would like to propose a toast to the Parson men and Tommy."

We all raise our mugs and drink deeply, allowing the warm liquid to slide down our throats and into our cores. It appears we all needed this. Our guests' level of concern and relief mirroring back at us surprises me, more intimate than it should have been for business partners.

Maggie refills our mugs and pours a heavier amount of whiskey this time—evidence she is celebrating too and in the only way we know how. I get up to help her. We still have not made eye contact or said a single word since my return.

While cleaning up the kitchen behind her as she boils more water, I quietly start, "Maggie, I am sorry for what I said before."

"I know. Me too." She puts her hands on the counter and braces herself, her head hung with fatigue. "Ellie, I was so scared for you, for us. I want to be strong but this place... it feels like it is closing in on me."

Setting down the rag, I walk over to her. "It's just the snow. We'll be better at rationing our food. Everyone will be better off now. Things will go back to the way they were."

"I'm not sure I want it to go back to the way things were." A hot tear falls from her face and hits the wood, staining it dark.

This statement punches me in the gut—the weight of its meaning setting in. Now is not the time to unpack this; mentally, I stuff it down. I want to distract Maggie from this.

"Where do you think they will stay?" I say, tipping my head in our guests' general direction.

She wipes her face and composes herself. "I reckon they stay here."

Daddy made a simple loft in the barn with a few cots and a wash basin to rent out to travelers for extra coins. Even the Parson men did not get a free night in the simple space. I figure that's where they will stay.

"I will move out of Momma and Daddy's room and let them have it. We can bring in one of the cots and one can use the sofa," Maggie says definitively.

This catches me off guard. It is improper for men to share a house with unmarried women. Momma would have been appalled.

Maggie's virtue and beauty are all she has left, and if she wants off this mountain, we can't sully her reputation. But before I can state this, Maggie walks over to where the rest sit comfortably together.

"Tommy, will you go and get one of the cots from the loft? You three will be staying in here with us," Maggie announces to everyone as she collects the mugs.

Tommy's eyes go wide, and he looks from Daniel to Graham for assistance.

Graham jumps in gracefully for Tommy. "We do not want to put you out. The loft will be fine for all of us."

"Nonsense. You are our guests and heroes. You will stay in here." Maggie continues cleaning up as if we are just talking about an everyday occurrence.

Her statement makes me cringe. I didn't want to be saved. I should've done better paired with her insisting these men sleep under our roof is too much for me.

Daniel stands up. "It is no trouble at all, Miss Maggie. We don't mind it out there."

Maggie's face steels up. "If you will not stay in here with us, I will take it as a personal insult. You will not be welcome back here, and we will no longer do business with you."

My jaw drops to the floor. Everyone goes silent.

Daniel clears his throat and says, "I would not dream of offending you. We will be most gracious to take you up on your hospitality."

Maggie curtly nods her head. "Now that is settled, Tommy, go get the extra cot, and everyone can wash up for dinner."

"Miss Maggie, if you don't mind, I would like to stay out in the loft," Tommy says tentatively. Then quickly adds, "I mean no offense by it. I just have twelve brothers and sisters, and having a whole area to myself would be a real treat."

"Fine then, but you will take extra blankets and make sure the fire stays roaring the whole time you are here. You understand?" She's eyeing him with motherly sternness that even I would follow without hesitation.

"Yes, ma'am," Tommy says respectfully. His rosy lips part into a wide sparkling adolescent smile. He leaves to start the fire and settle into his own space.

Daniel takes Lottie and follows Maggie into the kitchen. Looking at Graham, I see his eyes are as wide with shock as mine.

We start to laugh. I shrug and salute a silent cheer, and then we drain the rest of our mugs in unison. I will let this go for now. With the weather being so bad, we don't have to worry about the gossip for now.

Maggie does have a stubborn side, and admiration for it rushes over me. She is beginning to change, and this is just one instance I have noticed more recently. An uneasiness about this pokes at me, unsure how to feel about it all. But as I take in the warmness and laughter that fills the room, I finally allow a bud of hope for the future of our little orphaned family.

CHAPTER 13

It felt as if the mountains and our little cabin audibly exhaled once we knew we were not alone. The Parson men and Tommy became a constant in our lives. Reluctantly, we all said our goodbyes on a clear winter morning one week later. However, this was only goodbye for a little while. Graham, Daniel, and Tommy would all visit more frequently. Sometimes it was just Graham, or both Parson men, or Graham and Tommy. But Graham always came, and I was getting used to it.

The snowfall slows and thaws and eventually can't keep up with the spring sun. Graham makes the trip every week since that first visit. He nor Daniel ever sleep in the barn again and none of us ever discuss a different arrangement.

During the current visit, both Parson men decide to make the trek and leave their mercantile back in town for Tommy to manage. Their trading routes and business are really beginning to prosper, and Tommy is now taking on more responsibility.

Staying close to hunt, fish, and trap becomes more of a habit but is no longer necessary. Relaxing into moments of ease, knowing Daniel was with my sister, is the relief my tight shoulders need.

Graham and I ride together, alternating between a slow canter, trot, and full-out races depending on our energy. We pass the time by panning for gold, setting up traps, and tracking animals. He is becoming part of our lives—my life. I finally have everything I want. My sisters are safe and fed. Graham and Daniel are friends and a part of our lives; the shop is flourishing.

This new sense of serenity, however, is still met with a pang of guilt. We have not heard of Daddy's whereabouts for months. Mountain folk jaw on about seeing him before the snow flew, but nothing since.

The pebbles crunch under the weight of Gunpowder's hooves, which takes me back to a time when the leaves were turning yellow and orange, curling, and crusting. A time when I could see my breath on the fall air.

* * *

Daddy took me out to pan gold that day. He had shown me before, but today felt different. By the time I turned thirteen years old, he had given me more and more independence. Always a little too early, in my opinion, leaving me uncomfortable and unsure.

"That's when you grow the most, girl," he would say.

We headed deeper into the woods where the river slowed down. He had his rusty gold panning shovel slung over his shoulder and walked ahead of me in silence. We both could go for hours without talking and still feel comfortable together.

We got to a clearing along the bank of the river, and he speared his shovel into the dirt. He pointed to the shallow pebbled riverbed. The edges were covered in foliage browning and blackening from the cold. It looked deeper because the bank dropped off where it would rise again in the spring.

"See, Ellie, the water is slower here. We will start to dig and pan close to the bank. If the current is too fast and high, it throws the gold all over so you can't find any patterns—no pockets." He sloshed into the river to start.

I had my own shovel and followed him in.

He reached into his left breast coat pocket and pulled out his flask always close to his heart. He drank deeply and handed it to me. He only shared it when he was in the best of moods; this was a good sign. His bearded face and deep brown eyes smiled at me as I handed the flask back. We were going to have a good day.

We worked for nearly an hour in silence. These days were my favorite. It's when we connected the most.

Just as we were about to move along up the river to reposition, several sets of thundering hooves approached us from behind. Mr. Clancy and his gang rumbled to a stop. I knew Mr. Clancy's son, Logan. He was trouble just like his daddy was what Maggie always said, but I liked Logan enough. Mostly because he was the only kid who could run as fast as me, other than Graham but he wasn't around that much.

"Hey ya, Bill. You busy?" Mr. Clancy hollered from his horse to Daddy.

Daddy stuck his shovel in the ground and walked over. "What can I do yah for?"

"We've got some business to attend to—some of our cattle got out. We could use an extra hand."

I was confused. I knew where their cabin was, and I had never seen any cattle around. I knew they didn't even have a pasture. One of the local ranchers would drive their cattle into the woods for grazing at times, but I had never seen Mr. Clancy or any of his boys with any of their own.

My senses clicked into attention, observing for other clues about this suspicious situation. The other rougher men flanked Mr. Clancy. Big jugs of toxic-looking liquid sloshed around and candy-cane-shaped hook irons peeked out of their side saddles. Only cattle rustlers carried these tools—acid and running irons.

Daddy eyed the men then turned back to me. "Okay, Ellie, now you know what to do. I got you started. You're gonna stay here and do this on your own. I have some business with the boys. I want *you* to figure out where the vein would be. Like I've shown you before."

I looked around nervously, shifting my eyes between him and the men waiting for him. I didn't want him to go or get mixed up in some trouble.

"Daddy, I don't know if I'll remember how to do it all." I tried to get him to stay.

He narrowed his eyes at me and asked, "So you haven't been listening to me then?"

"No, sir. I've been listenin', but what if I can't find any here and have to move on?"

"I'll find yah. You think you can find that vein for me before I get back?" He smiled at me, knowing I would rise to a challenge.

I took the bait; I wanted to make him proud. "I will."

"Just keep going until I come back, you hear?" He handed me the flask one more time, and I drank three large gulps greedily. I wanted him to have his wits about him; he needed a sharper head than I did so I tried to drain the rest of the liquid down my throat as fast as I could. The other men's deep laughs thundered around me but I didn't care. Daddy grabbed the flask from my lips and out of my hand, causing me to lose a little down my chin.

"Whoa, El, save some for me."

I knew I wouldn't see him for hours. We both tipped our hats to each other, and I watched him skulk away. The brown liquor was warming me from the inside as I pulled my leather jacket in tighter and looked down at the river running by. I thought I might find what Daddy had been looking for all these years. Then he wouldn't have to run around with that good-for-nothin' Clancy Gang.

Daddy's motto was, "There is gold in this river but we have to find the big strike or it ain't worth nothing."

He was never satisfied with the nuggets we had found so far so he would throw them back and say, "We aren't there yet."

Today would be different. I shoved my shovel into the sand and scooped up a half worth just like he showed me to put into my pan with a wet splash. I could already see the shiny specs in it but nothing really caught my eye. Taking the pan into my hands, I stepped into the water. The water was cold but not icy thanks to the whiskey coursing through me.

Sloshing the pan from side to side, adding water little by little to wash away the pebbles and sand, I only saw a few specs and knew this wasn't anything to get excited about. Dumping it back into the river, I looked up at the bend.

The birds were chirping, and the day really was a pretty one. This type of day was cool in the morning, warm during the day, and then crisp at night—my favorite kind of day. I still didn't know which direction to take so I just took a few steps deeper into the river and dug in. Again, I came up with specs. I repeated this over and over again for half the morning.

The day was warming me up, so I took off my coat and drank deeply from my canteen. By then, my buzz was strong. I wished I had more whiskey to keep it going. I removed my hat and wiped my hair out of my face. I sifted through yet another section of earth and then I saw it—one nugget shining through the muddy water. It easily separated from the muck. It was the size of a small pea but it was the biggest one I had seen yet. I tucked it into my left breast jacket pocket, over my heart, just like Dad would do with his flask. I marked the spot with a stake and then continued.

Walking deeper into the water, I scooped up more earth as the water quickly sloshed up to my thighs. I carried it over to the banks and poured it into my pan. I sifted through again. I saw two nuggets the size of the last one and my heart leaped out of my chest. I was doing it. I threw those bits back and kept heading north. I dug in again and this time found four nuggets. Then five.

Then, I dug in deeper, pulled up a full shovel blade, and dumped it into my pan. Sloshing the mud away little by little, my little muscles not used to the extra weight, I nearly dropped the whole thing twice but somehow kept it steady. Then, there it was, the biggest shiniest nugget I had ever seen. Daddy had never shown me one this big. Holding it up to my little finger, it was about the same size as Daddy's thumb.

Shaking all over, my mind raced to the possibility. This could be it. I knew I could find more, do more, and keep going. Maybe a bigger one was close, maybe just this next shovel. The same pan held six other pea-sized nuggets, and I pocketed all of them. My treasures were precious to me.

The sun was starting to fall over the horizon, and the colors dimmed to dusk. I had been here all day. It was nearly time to head home for dinner, but I had not seen any signs of Daddy. He'd told me to stay out here until he returned.

I had not stopped to eat, distracted by the buzz from this morning and the excitement brimming inside of me. The little sparks of energy I received with each nugget propelled me to keep going, distracting me from hunger until now. I could now understand why Daddy was so obsessed with finding gold. It almost gave me the same kind of distraction that drinking gave me.

Daddy had always compared sex and gambling as being "pretty damn good too" when it came to this kind of feeling, but I didn't know anything about those things.

So now I had a new way to get my fix—another thing that took me out of my mind. Daddy must be coming back soon, and when he did, I was going to show him my big nugget.

Continuing up the river and stepping back into the water, I cringed as the iciness hit me again. Resting had cooled me down, and this time of year the heat from the day did not linger long after the sun started to set. Still, I kept going. I kept finding nuggets that were the same size. More and more of them.

I clenched my jaw to keep my teeth from chattering. I didn't care. I would just do one more scoop, sift one more pan, and pocket one more nugget. My heart was racing and my fingertips were burning from the cold, but I did not care.

My whole body was still vibrating from the cold and the anticipation. I had found five nuggets, and my coat pocket was fat from smaller gold pieces. Shoving the wooden stake deep into the ground, I looked up to see the darkness that had crept over the woods and the brush moving from the night animals waking.

I was about to head home when I looked up again and out stumbled Daddy. He looked determined and walked straight for me.

"You, still here, huh?" His words slurred.

"Yes, you told me to stay until you got back so I did, and look what I got." It wasn't the vein but maybe this would be enough to make him happy. It might be the motivation we needed for tomorrow when we could really work together and make progress. I pulled open my coat and exposed my bounty to him. He peered in. My chest swelled, waiting to tell him all about my day. I was getting colder as I stood there waiting for him. My stomach growled.

"Girl, dump it out so I can see it."

I peeled my coat off, and he held the pan out in front of me. I turned out my pocket and the nuggets clinked, making pattering sounds as they made the connection.

He bounced them around, assessing their weight and shine. I waited in suspense for his response, never truly sure what it would be. Again, my body shook.

His eyes shot to me. "Why did you keep all these little bits?"

Stepping back, I replied, "They are the biggest I've ever seen. There must be more where they came from."

His eyes narrowed. "I told you, we are not looking for little bits. We are only looking for the big 'ens."

"I know. I just thought it would add up over time, you know, like how the others do it." I knew other people made a good steady income from what I found today.

"I told you, it ain't what *we're* lookin' fer." His nostrils flared, and his dark eyes widened.

I watched him dump them into his hand and drop the pan on the ground with a large clank at our feet. He sneered at the pile in his hand then cocked his arm back, throwing them all back into the water.

"I will not beg for people to weigh my gold dust. I told you, if the nuggets are not the size of your palm, you do not keep them. It ain't called dusting for gold. It's called striking gold, and striking gold means striking *big*."

My shoulders sagged as my whole day's work was flung away, easily and simply discarded. My rage was a quick rise and sudden blast. I picked up the gold pan and flung it into the river; it sank to the bottom quickly.

Spinning around, fuming, and seeing red, my buzz completely gone, I had a headache now. "You've never done any better."

Our eyes met and held. He was at me in two steps. He pulled up his hand and backhanded me. My ears rang as I involuntarily turned my body away. The heat inside me blasted. Picking up the shovel, I swung it at him hard. The shovel made contact with his stomach, and he stepped back, gasping for air. He had nearly toppled over, tripping over his shovel and clumsy feet.

He picked up the other shovel, and we circled each other. The handles of our shovels clanked together. He was smiling and sweating. I attacked him like a knight in a battle, and he countered my every move. His foot sank stupidly into the pebbly riverbed, and he stepped into the icy water. I used the tip of my shovel to throw him off balance, and I heard him splash into the water.

I dropped my shovel and ran.

Daddy was swearing in the water, splashing around, trying to right himself, and yelling all the cuss words I knew.

"Fuck you, Ellie. You good for nothing girl. You better fuckin' run."

I sprinted all the way home. Bursting into the cabin, I peeled off my coat and threw it onto the floor. I slammed my body down into the wooden chair nearest to the fire. My pulse pounded in my ears and over the cheek that still stung. My mother and Maggie stood there in silence.

Momma asked, "Honey, are you okay?"

My breath was still rapid, and my lungs were burning. The warmth of the cabin was stuffy, and my wet clothes were getting heavy and tightening around me.

"Yeah, Momma, I'm fine. Daddy and I got into a fight. I pushed him into the river. I didn't stick around to see if he was fine. I hit him with my shovel."

"Oh, Ellie, you and your temper," clucked Maggie.

My eyes narrowed, and I shot at her, "He hit me first."

My stomach started to coil back up and prepare for another fight. My face became puffy and red as a bruise started to form. Maggie knew better and looked down.

My mother rushed over to me and helped me out of my wet clothes. She hung a blanket around my shoulders and found something dry for me to wear. She then fixed my plate with the dinner I missed. The warmth in my hands and toes was returning.

Daddy's boots stomped up on the porch. My fork and knife still close, I instinctively reached out for both of them.

He swung open the door and looked at me. He had both shovels, the pan, and our riffles in his arms. He was soaking wet. I braced myself for another round.

My mother stepped in front of him. "Bill, honey, you look so cold."

She took the items out of his arms and set them down one by one, trying to prolong the time she stood in between us. He looked at her and all he could see was her now. Momma was about the only thing that could soften him.

I stayed where I was and waited. Momma then tilted to the side and laced her arm through Daddy's arm as she ushered him toward the fire. She tended to him the same way she had with me. He peeled his clothes off, and she gave him another warm blanket she kept close to the fire.

Turning my head, I looked at him and our eyes met. He had a bit of a sparkle to his eyes that told me he was no longer as mad. I knew that fuse was still short and the smallest spark could reignite it.

He looked over to the kitchen. "It smells good. Is there any left for me?"

I rolled my eyes because of course there would be. Momma smiled to herself and loaded up his plate with venison, potatoes, and crusty bread. She tactfully placed his spot at the opposite end of the table from where I sat. She always positioned us this way to keep as much distance as possible between us.

Daddy pulled out his flask and the jar of whiskey, and my mother put a glass down next to it. He poured a heavy amount and lifted his glass to me, his version of a truce. I nodded my head and continued to eat.

We ate in silence for a while. I finished my plate but remained in my seat so as not to draw attention to myself. I waited until he was done and then went to get up. Daddy cleared his throat and then threw something heavy onto the table. It rumbled over itself to me. It was the largest of the nuggets I found from today; he hadn't thrown it back.

"Look what Ellie found," he told the rest of them.

My sister and momma huddled in closer and looked at it. Maggie picked it up and inspected it, and her eyes went wide.

"I have never seen one this big," she whispered. I observed everyone warily.

My mother looked over Maggie's shoulder and wrapped her arm around her. "Ellie, you found this?"

My shoulders dropped and relaxed.

"It's not what we are looking for but it is a damn good start." Daddy motioned for Momma to come over to him.

I was beaming.

I sat up taller. "It took me all day just to find some bits, but I am sure if I had more time, I could find more."

Momma's eyes, warm and welcoming, met mine as she settled in next to her husband. "I know you can."

Daddy stood up suddenly and took the nugget out of Maggie's hand to place it in mine. "Remember, this isn't what we are looking for but it might be a good reminder for you. It'll remind you of the feeling it gave you when you found it. It will drive you to want to look for more and more and then when we strike it big, you will remember how little this was in comparison to what we could find."

I looked up at him and smiled. Turning over the nugget in my hand, I admired its gleam and knobby edges. I held it tightly to my chest and got up to go to bed.

"Oh, and Ellie..." I turned to him slowly as he spoke. "If you ever come at me with a shovel again, your ass will be so sore, you won't be able to sit for a week." I knew this reunion was too good to be true.

* * *

Graham's deep booming tone brings me back to the summer day.

"Hey, Ellie, want to take a swim?" Graham calls out to me.

His knowing eyes scan me, almost as if he is checking to see if I am okay. Relaxing my lids and releasing the muscles in my face, I'm attempting to mask the eddy of emotions I've just experienced. Sadness, anger, nostalgia—it's all there.

All the hiking and trapping has us working up a sweat, and the day is warmer than we expected; we've overdressed for the occasion.

Graham is already removing his layers.

Squinting my eyes, I burst out in a devilish smile. "I'll race you."

He flashes his full-face Graham smile, and I giggle. This noise catches me off guard. *I don't fucking giggle.* Realizing that he is already ahead of me, my competitive nature kicks in.

Stripping down to our undergarments as we had as children, we race to the water. He grabs me around the midsection and throws me back behind him. Sprinting to catch up, I jump on his back, and we topple into the cold water as one.

"*Ahhhh,* it's freezing!" I chatter.

"Jesus, El, when did you get so soft?" He splashes water at me. Somehow his teasing doesn't sting.

CHAPTER 14

Splashing and forgetting we are no longer children, Graham over judges our proximity as he grabs my wrist and pulls me into him. We are closer now than we have ever been; my body and mind register it. Splashing in our undergarments was a summer pastime. We've done this together so many times, yet now it's different somehow.

Water beads off his wet dark brown hair and drips down his face and over his lips. He shakes his head and showers my face. He restrains me closer as I feign like I want to escape his grasp.

His arm wraps around my shoulders and then under my legs. I am flush against his chest and his breathing deepens with mine. As we wade there, his body begins shaking from the cold, and his lips are starting to go blue. I'm sure mine are too. He cradles me in his arms and carries me out weightless from the water and then effortlessly continues to exit with me in his arms onto dry land. Our eyes never lose connection.

He finally lowers me to my own two legs that wobble unsteadily. Stepping back, his eyes only break from mine to rove over my entire body, slowly, deliberately—seeing all of me. I feel too exposed and go to cover myself. Reaching out with a firm grip, he stops me and pulls me into him, reconnecting our gaze. We are inches apart. His head tilts and starts to lean in. His grip on my wrists lightens and then slides up, over my palms until our hands are intertwined.

The sound of hooves approaching breaks our trance. I wiggle to get out of his arms.

Out of the woods appears Logan, Tricia, and their posse. I am instantly aware we are in our delicates and the fabric is clinging to me, leaving no need for imagination.

"Whoa, Graham. I wasn't sure Ellie here would ever let any of us take her clothes off." Ice and jealousy slice across Logan's words.

"Ellie took her own clothes off," Graham defends as I run behind Gunpowder.

"We aren't complaining. El, I knew a beautiful figure was hidden under all that leather." Logan stretches his scruffy thick neck to steal another peek at me.

Tricia chimes in, "Yeah, I half thought there would be man bits between your legs with how pious you are. And with this pretty boy Graham? Really, Ellie?"

They all laugh. I keep quiet and try to push into my dry clothes but everything is sticking, and I can't get them on.

"Hey, Graham, how long will you be staying this time? I heard Katie and you were getting cozy at church. I bet she's missing you with how much time you've been spending in *our* parts." Logan clearly emphasizes Graham was not one of us; Graham is in Logan's territory.

Tricia rides closer to Graham, her eyes taking a slow trip to gaze below his waist. "I wouldn't mind getting to know you better. I am so used to the rough hands of these men. It would be a good chance to feel the softness of a merchant's son for once. I bet he pays better, too."

Tricia licks her lips. That does it for me. No longer caring that they see me, I stomp out and stand right next to Graham. Still dripping wet, I grab his hand and lace our fingers together.

"You all have a problem with this?" I challenge.

Logan looks hurt but then puffs out a laugh. "No, El. We don't have a problem with it at all. Just come see me when city boy here gets boring or when he gets sick of your hillbilly ways." His gaze lazily drifts to my translucent chest and hard nipples for all to see. I lift them to emphasize I don't give a damn.

"Hey, slick, maybe if you treated women better, you might be surprised how your company could improve." Graham's calm tone clearly and smoothly insults them all in one swift slap of the tongue.

Logan's eyes and nostrils flare. "Come on, guys, let's leave Ellie and Graham alone. It's about time Ellie becomes a woman anyhow."

Graham drops my hand and takes off after Logan on foot. Logan laughs cruelly and kicks his horse to go. Tricia and the rest of them take off after him, glaring as they ride off.

I am now pissed and freezing. We both dress behind our horses, discarding the undergarments to dry behind the protection of our horses, our moment lost.

Back on the horses riding together, we are both silent and simmering from that encounter. To go from being in Graham's arms to fighting with Logan's gang, my heart is still pounding.

"Who is Katie?" I snap.

"Katie is no one. She is a town girl who thinks she fancies me," he says, looking straight ahead.

"Bullshit. All those women fancy you." Now that I have seen him nearly completely naked, I can see why.

"That doesn't mean I fancy them," he replies matter-of-factly.

Puffing out a laugh, I doubt it. "So, you are telling me you don't like any of those fancy girls?"

"There is only one. There has only ever been one."

My head snaps to look at him. "Stop, Graham. Just stop it, okay? I don't have time for this. I have my sisters to take care of. I don't have the energy to think about anything extra. So just go settle down with nice, pretty Katie and leave me alone." I want to push him away and keep him at a safer distance.

I want to be like a bird in the distance who gives you the privilege to observe the articulation of her wings, allowing the admirer a more intimate gaze. Knowing she was never in any real danger, she gives the illusion you may just have a chance to touch her smooth feathers. This behavior made the most sense. It is safer this way.

"I like trouble." His blue eyes bore into me.

"Gah, insufferable! I warned you." Kicking Gunpowder, I ride off.

My annoyance shifts to playfully competitive against my will as he catches up to me and flashes me his smile. That Goddamned smile. We race all the way back to the cabin where Maggie will be fixing dinner by now.

Graham and I enter the cabin, laughing and verbally sparring when I notice how close Maggie and Daniel are. She is leaning over the counter, and he is on the other side, inches away from her face. They jump back as if a spark dropped between them.

Tilting my head, I make eye contact with Maggie, sending her a silent question. *What was that about?* Their closeness throws me off.

She ignores it. "Who's ready for dinner?"

CHAPTER 15

Graham's presence encourages my guts to stop their incessant churning and eases the tightness with each visit. The peace and comfort are unsettlingly foreign.

Catching my mind wandering to Graham is something I have to keep recovering from. Out hunting this afternoon is no different. I should be focusing on this task, not on his dark blue eyes, their intensity, and their ability to see through me. It's madding.

Shaking my head, I scan the clearing for movement. Good thing thoughts do not make noise because mine are loud and demanding. I'm oscillating between enjoying my summer with Graham and wanting him to leave me alone. I have enough to think about without him taking up all this space. Besides, it won't work out in the end. His interest in me will fade once he realizes I won't ever be his little wife. He deserves that, and it's not who I am.

He hasn't been around this week yet, and I am missing him. *Damn it, I don't want to miss him but there it is.* I just do.

Maggie spent so much time with Daniel while Graham and I were out doing what we do best—hunting. I hope Maggie isn't growing tired of Daniel. The Parson men are a package deal. They run their trading routes together because the bandits and natives could look at their large cart and think they could score easily. I feel sorry for the men who thought they would get away with anything other than a black eye or a hole through the chest.

Graham is a sharpshooter; he learned by his daddy's side. Graham is impressive with a gun, a knife, and his hands. Those hands.

The fact that he is a better shot than me and just barely beats me at everything ruffles my feathers. It also keeps me interested, to be honest, and I think he knows that. He doesn't go easy on me. Not now, and not back when we were kids. We used to run races, shoot guns, and wrestle. At first, when we were little, the games were evenly won. Yet when we got older, he pulled ahead of me just by a hair. Not everything or every time, but more and more frequently.

Again, I try and refocus my mind on the task at hand. But because my mind is elsewhere, I miss the approaching footsteps. I'm not aware of another's presence until his rough hand skims lightly across my low back—over my exposed skin.

Turning my head, I jump, registering his body lying next to mine. I can't help when my lips involuntarily turn up in a coy smile but silently scold myself for being distracted by him when he was and wasn't here. This thing between us is exposing me, making me as vulnerable as the soft belly of a porcupine.

I reach back to pull my tunic down over my exposed skin, and he pouts.

"I was enjoying the view, El." Knowingly, he teases me.

"Bet you were," I joust back.

He knows I need to get a kill today so his gaze focuses ahead of us.

I hate that I crave his hand to find my back again.

"Nothing yet?" Graham asks as he surveys the woods in front of us.

"I have not checked my traps today but I wanted to try to shoot something before I did my rounds," I reason out loud tactfully.

"Let's start to make the rounds. I bet we will run into something on the way." He rises onto his muscled and tanned forearms, raising from the ground before I respond.

He sees my eyes rove over those hands and forearms automatically, and he returns it with direct eye contact. The intensity sets in as he scans down and then back up my body to meet my eyes again. He flashes his big warm smile with a twinge of youthful mischief, and my core tightens. *Shit, fuck,* I do not have room for this.

We set off on foot, not bringing our horses this time. We hike in silence in a way I have never done with anyone else other than Daddy. Somehow, it's different, though. I'm calmer, less easily startled. Being this at ease makes me nervous, though. What's wrong with me? We created this rhythm together that needs no words; just movements and counter-movements.

Graham touches my elbow and motions his head to where the trees are the thickest. My eyes adjust to the darkness of the woods and almost instantly find what he's directing my attention to.

Tightening my body, I raise my gun to my chin and take quick aim. The bang of the gun ricochets off the silent valley, dropping the doe instantly. Birds take flight from my noise. Graham mimics my actions and takes down two fat pheasants.

As one unit, we'll feast tonight. Our eyes meet again; tension laces the air and not just because of our kills. The adrenaline still pulses through my veins.

"And just like that, dinner is served," he says with a pleased, *I told you so,* look on his face.

"Don't look so smug. I was about to get up and go anyway. You snuck up on me just in time. We could've missed each other."

"I would've found you." His response is dripping with manly arrogance and confidence.

"Who said I wanted you to?" I stand my ground as he steps in closer. My body betrays me, allowing this to happen, a subtle challenge. My mind knows the trouble and pain that would follow but my body doesn't care. He'll be gone on another route soon, and I am not a woman who'll pine for any man.

"Ellie, why do you make it so hard on me?" I see his lower lip quirk into a smile again. Not the big Graham smile that forced me to smile back but a preview of the main show.

"Because you men all want the same thing. A little wifey who cooks, cleans, and has babies. That just isn't me." I take off to collect my kill, not wanting to have this conversation again.

He follows me and again; I sense his presence creep up on me.

Turning to face off with him defensively, I grunt, "Why are you always so close?"

I realize we are dangerously close this time since he did not anticipate this about-face.

He looks down at me as my neck cranes up at him; he does not back away.

"Because I want you, Ellie. I have always wanted you," he says deeply, simply, as if this is mere fact.

"You don't want me—not really, Graham. You can have your fun with me where no one can see. But I will never be what you need. In your world, back in town, you wouldn't want anything to do with me," I say as I lower my chin and turn away.

"I don't give a damn what anyone would say."

Puffing out a laugh, I brush him off. "You have your routes and life down there. I have the shop and my sisters to take care of. Our life together would never work."

"It could if you wanted it to. You would be great on the road. I think you would love it," he says as if this was even a fathomable option.

We just let them into our lives; he's now talking about me going with him—leaving here? I've had enough.

"Ha! You will end up with some lovely lady who wears lace and dresses and fawns all over you." I swat my hand in dismissal. "Listen, I am either destined to be alone or I'll settle for one of these roughnecks. They're my people. At least they know who I am and accept it. You come from soft beds and full bellies; we come from grit and dirt. That's where I'll end up. I've made peace with that. Why can't you?"

"Ellie, you think you are one of these scumbags but you're not. You are used to people like Logan and Tricia? Your people? They would sooner cut you down with their tongues, or in Tricia's case, literally stab you in the back and laugh about it as you bleed out," Graham retorts. "You think their harsh words and banter are admiration, but it's a way to keep you feeling like trash just like them. You think if a person treats you badly, they are one of you. You act like it's something you should be proud of."

Those words stop me in my tracks. *How dare he.*

"At least my people say it to your face. Yours slap their tongues with gossip behind your back." My anger is starting to boil. He has no idea what it means to be a part of this world. We could never work.

"You think those guys will give you what you want? Really, El?" His eyes demand something from me that I'm not ready to give.

"You don't know what I want," I reply, slinging my retort in his face and turning my body to stomp away.

My hand makes its way to hoist the gun back to my shoulder when Graham's thick, rough, muscled hand reaches out and stops it.

Graham pulls me to his body and grabs my other hand.

"You want a partner. Someone you can rely on. Someone who you can trust and who stands up for you. You want a man who is not ashamed of you and understands the responsibilities you have. Who accepts you for all you are. You want someone who challenges you and pushes you to be better. But all you have known is harsh words, and you've been let down so much you only know people who treat you like shit."

His words slap me in the face. How is he so right and so infuriating? I rip away from his hold.

"Graham, you think you want this now because it is new and exciting, but eventually you'll want something different."

"Ellie, you are so wrong. You are all I've ever wanted, and you better get used to that." I can't ignore the sincerity in his deep velvety voice.

Fuck, my body responds before my mind and logic catch up. Launching ourselves at the other, our lips crushing together in a savage urgency, our tongues making up for the lost time.

His steady grip on my waist lifts my tunic. His calluses scrape across my belly and my core tightens, shooting heat between my legs.

He lowers his lips to the curve of my jaw and then makes a trail down the soft tissue along my neck. I tip my head back to allow him more access as a moan escapes my lips. Graham releases pressure enough so I can feel his wide smile graze my collar.

Releasing my gun and then lifting my arms, he removes my tunic completely and discards it on the forest floor. He slows the pace and takes a step back. He is actually admiring me, taking me all in. I love it but it also sends my nerves scattering. He keeps his hands on my hips but takes in my naked top and intensifies his gaze.

"I have waited years for this, Ellie. You're better than I could ever imagine."

His lips then make their way across my breasts as my nipples harden beneath his strong and deliberate kisses. The air is cooler now as the sun dips and goosebumps flit across my body.

I start to shake, not because of the temperature but because of the anticipation. Like he always has, he picks up on my response and pulls me closer to reassure and warm me.

Reaching for his shirt, I lift it faster than he did with mine. I want to touch his skin *now*.

His chiseled abs peek out first. I have seen these exquisite muscles before but I've never dared to touch them until now. My fingertips graze up to his chest and then back down to where his waist V's into his pants.

His nimble fingers loosen and swiftly remove my pants first and then his. The leathers fall away from our bodies at the same time. Our gazes devour the bare skin and then our mouths follow where our eyes have the privilege of feasting first.

Graham picks me up, his hands under my cheeks, and I wrap my legs around his midsection. He is strong and ready for me. Careful to find a soft spot, he lowers me down gently and expertly. His mouth is back on mine and then starts to travel down my body again in a tantalizingly slow meandering pace, teasing and pausing. His warm wet tongue forges the trail.

Painfully, he stops just before he is between my legs. Lifting my head to see what made him pause, I take in the wide grin painted across his face and the light in his stormy eyes. He maintains eye contact as he plunges his tongue where I want it most, the residual smile grazing my most delicate places. The apex of my legs was ready.

Continuing to use his tongue, he makes circles and soft licks right where I am the most sensitive, taking his time there. I prop up on my elbows and enjoy the view. His dark mess of hair tips back and forth the way I had fantasized about it before. His arms wrap around my legs, holding my thighs in a wider stance. The broadness of his back nestles between me and is the sexiest thing I've ever seen, followed by his sculpted ass.

As he continues to lap at me and drive me closer and closer to completion, he dips a single finger deliciously, slowly, inside of me, taking his time and using steady strokes. My hips buck up to meet his pressure.

"You like that. Don't you?" He moans and murmurs against my wet flesh, almost sending me over the edge.

"Ahhhh, Graham, I want you," I plead.

"Ellie, you have me." The confidence and arrogance plunge me over the edge.

I can't help the convulsions he releases from me. My mind is only here and only with him. A moment of freedom. Nothing else matters but this moment.

"Is this what I have been missing all these years?" I ask breathlessly.

"There is more where that came from," he says wryly.

We continue to roll around, kissing and devouring. We have always been competitive, and love-making is no different. First me, then him, then us.

We lie there under the stars now, listening to the night wake up. Graham pulls his fur coat over the top of us, and we gaze up at the little white dots dusted across the sky.

This changes everything, and I'm not sure I'm ready for it.

CHAPTER 16

The days of summer stretch out in a glorious way. Life is finally ticking at a manageable pace. Deeper breaths come more easily, almost naturally. Almost. Not just because the sun graces us with its presence for longer, warmer, and more abundant days but because I spend my time hunting, fishing, panning, and making love with Graham. I've reluctantly allowed this relationship to happen even though the voice in the back of my head warns me each time I open up to Graham. *This is too good to be true.*

I'm still not convinced this thing we have will work out long-term. Deep in my core, I hold the belief Graham wants a wife and homemaker, which will never be me.

He won't want a wanton woman forever. He will grow tired of this wildness. I could never be with a townie. There's no place for us to be together unless he stays out here. I shut that last hopeful thought down. I know Graham has responsibilities and ultimately, he'll choose them just like I'll choose mine. But, just for now, I block out this issue altogether.

Graham is visiting by himself this time. Maggie seems to make herself and Lottie scarce when he arrives solo so we can have more time to ourselves.

"Ellie, darlin'. Come here." Graham reaches a hand out and then beckons me to come closer with one finger, the same one that had just caressed me in places that made my toes curl. He always has a way of pulling me out of my head and back to him.

It's well into the night. We had sex in the living room, on the sofa, on the fur rug in front of the fire, and somehow have made it back to the sofa. His lap is covered with a blanket but it still doesn't conceal the evidence that he wants me... again.

Briefly, I run to the kitchen to fetch two glasses of water. Naked except for a thick gray blanket draped over my shoulders, I filled the glasses unashamed as he watched me.

Padding over, I climb on his lap and straddle him. I allow the blanket to open and fall to my hips so he can see me completely. The warmth of the fire on my back and the blanket keep me plenty comfortable.

I want to tease him, so I make sure the blanket between us is pinned down with my knees, not allowing our skin to touch. Using the blocked friction, I begin to rotate my hips.

He groans and pulls me closer. Graham uses his hands to guide my face to his swollen, full lips and allows my rhythm to control the pace. We are both insatiable for the other.

Graham bites my bottom lip harder than he has before. The sharpness of it surprises me but instantly ignites my want—no, *need*—for him. Aggression springs out of me, and I press him hard against the sofa. Allowing my feral side out, I let myself loose on him. I grab a fist full of dark hair and force his head back so I can expose his neck the same way he did to me. Licks, nips, and kisses mimic my fingertip's trail.

Suddenly, Graham lifts me up by my up waist with one arm and rips out the barrier between us. Agonizingly slowly, he lowers me onto his ready length.

We are now one; he draws me in closer and whispers, "Ride me, El."

Slowly at first, I raise myself up and down the length of him with the muscles in my toned, tanned legs from our summer rides together. Bringing us to the edge of completion several times this way becomes my specialty, and we prefer the synchronicity of a dramatic climatic ending.

Graham uses the blanket to assist me, and we climb together. His hardness hits deep within me, knowing all the right places to purposely press. Reaching down, his rough fingertip somehow softens when it finds the apex of my legs. He tactfully teases the combination of external and internal sensations I need to have me nearly come undone around him, then and there.

At that moment, my pace hastens but he keeps his fingers moving devastatingly slowly in tiny circles, the contrasting paces keeping me glued to the here and now. It is like he knows my mind has a hard time shutting down, so distracting me with new pressure, pace, and position keeps me engaged completely, focused only on him.

His finger whispers over my most sensitive spot. I want to look into his eyes as I unravel so I grab his attention by rubbing my breasts against his lips, a maneuver I know will make him open his eyes. When they do, I allow his intense gaze to lock with mine, and that's all we needed to lose ourselves completely. I bite on my lower lip to stifle my cry and he does the same using my exposed shoulder as a gag, the slight pain intensifying my ending that much more.

We sit there as we both pulsate through the release. He holds me close as we both try to catch our breath. Graham plants soft kisses where his teeth had left little crescent marks. I settle into the crook of his neck; sleep would feel so sweet now. The soft strokes on my back lull me off to oblivion, sated in every way.

* * *

A large bang sounds as Tommy spills into the cabin, allowing the chill from the night to claw its way down my naked back. I am instantly awake.

"Tommy, what the hell?" Graham lifts the blanket over my shoulders to cover me. His body is in no need of modestly, apparently, since he stands up in all his wonder. Tommy can see every inch of him. Coolly, Graham picks up his pants and pulls them on.

Tommy's face is white—not with embarrassment but terror. Why is he here so late and now?

Tommy blurts out in a shaky voice, "Graham, there's been an accident. Your Daddy and I were on a route and his horse fell into a hole, throwing him off. Graham, it shattered his lower leg. I had to ride to town for help, and it took us hours to get him back. You need to come now."

Graham's eyes widen as his chest rises and falls rapidly. "Could you see bone, Tommy?" Graham asks as calmly as he can.

Casting his eyes down, Tommy replies, "Yes, just under his knee."

Maggie bursts into the room. "Tommy, what does he need?"

"Right now, he's asking for Graham." Tommy levels his eyes at Maggie.

Graham hurries to collect his stuff and then spins around to me.

"Ellie, I want you to come with me. Your sisters too." His blue, panicked eyes search mine for understanding. When I don't respond, he continues. "I don't know how long I will be gone, and I can't stand leaving you all up here alone."

It's going to be fall and then winter again; we have to plan better this time. There's still too much to do. But Graham is talking about us leaving it all behind. The shop and our claim on the land are all we have left of our parents. Momma's legacy, their dreams for us—all discarded to follow a man? The very thought of it would disgrace them both. There's no way I can do this to them.

"We can't go with you," I say with almost no volume at all.

Looking at Maggie's thin silhouette, her femininity and softness have me thinking about her honor. It's the only card she has left to secure a husband. It's still maintained at this point. I know the word has already gotten out that the Parson men were visiting often but it's something else entirely to stay with them in town. This is yet another reason why we can't go and be with the Parson men. My mind's quickly staking all the reasons why this isn't an option like a skilled mason would with bricks.

Graham grabs my shoulders. "Ellie, come with me. Your sisters can come tomorrow with Tommy."

"You know I won't do that." My stomach starts to make a lazy flip at first but then twists. This is why I didn't want to get involved. I knew it was too good to be true.

His worried eyes search for help from Maggie but she seems unsure of what to do.

I look over at Maggie who is quiet and appears to be calculating our options. Neither of us has left the mountain in years. This is our home, and we have never thought of leaving. Her closed-down pondering stance, the flicker of doubt flitting across her face, and her silence solidify my decision. Maggie has changed since our parents left but she still has their values. I know shacking up with an unmarried townie would disgrace our mother and all she had taught us.

"We'll come and visit," I say, making the final decision for us both, trying to sidestep and end this conflict.

"I don't want you to come and visit. I want you *all* to come and live with us." The desperation in his eyes cracks my heart open. "It's something my dad and I have been tossing around, and now it just makes sense."

Maggie's eyes widen. "Daniel wants us all to live there with him?"

Narrowing my eyes at my sister, I say, "Maggie you know that is not an option, especially for you."

Graham steps up to me, grabs my shoulders, and forces me to look up at him. "Ellie, you need to get off this mountain." His voice starts to tremble. "This place, these people, they'll break you."

The force of that comment hits me as if he kicked me in the chest. "This is our home. The people in it, the shop, our whole existence, are up here. People depend on us. The very peace depends on us."

"Ellie, if you don't leave here, it will slowly strip all that is good in you." Graham says this like we're having a completely new conversation. It seems like he's wanted to talk about this for a long time and the pressure of this emergency forces it all out. The sharp angle of this conversation throws me off.

"We are just fine up here. We appreciate all that you've done for us, but we will manage on our *own* now." I try and steer the conversation to a flippant closure, steeling myself up against what he just said. All the weight of it is too much for me to unpack just now.

"Ellie, my father is not calling me down to nurse him. He is calling me down to take over the route. He is hurt, and Tommy will have to run the shop." This means Graham won't even be down there with us. He'll be alone on the road.

I know the fall trading trip is coming up. They've been preparing for it for months but it isn't for a few more weeks. We should have had at least three more weeks before we had to have *this* conversation. I was planning to cut things off then. Not completely, but in an open way, releasing us both from any obligations over the winter months.

"I will be gone for months, and I want you to come with me." His eyes bore into the armor that I'm quickly covering my heart with.

"Was this something you were going to ask me to do before all this?" I say, leveling my voice to a dangerous and flat tone.

He runs a hand through his hair and looks to the ceiling. "Well, yes. God, Ellie, I was going to ask you soon but I know how you get with things like this."

"Because it is not a topic of discussion. I warned you but you didn't listen. Did you?" All the hope in my heart leaks out rapidly.

"This is no place for you or your sisters. Can't you see that?" His voice hardens with what I am sure is frustration and pain.

"I can see you have a family and business that need your attention, and I have one of my own." I try and dismiss him.

Maggie chimes in finally; I think she will back me and reassure Graham the way she does with Lottie when she is upset, but instead, she just turns on me. "Ellie, I think you should go with him."

Now I am starting to feel attacked. *Why is she not on my side?*

"That is not going to happen, Maggie," I say through gritted teeth and stalk to our room to put clothes on. I feel way too exposed.

Maggie is on my heels. "I think he's right. You need to get off this mountain, and I think this is our way out. Even if we don't go, you should."

Turning to her, my face stitches up. I'm tired of this conversation already. "The mountains are the only place I know, and I would never leave you. You have to know that."

Maggie scans my face, deciding not to argue with me any further. I dress quickly. She stays in the bedroom as I stalk back out to the living room. Tommy has left, and it's just Graham and me.

"Ellie, tell me why you fight this—what we have, the life we could build together?" He tries to use his eyes to move me but I am not brave enough to meet them.

"It was never meant to be. I told you from the beginning. You want something I can't give. You are from a different world—one I am not and will never be a part of. This is my home. Our family has a job to do, just like you and yours. It's our role; there is no changing the way things are. Without it or my sisters, I am nothing."

"When are you going to see that you are more than all this?" Graham motions around the room but he really means this mountain. My mountain.

Softness and sadness flicker across his eyes. I can see he believes I am something more. I had started to believe it for a moment but this is who I am and who I was raised to be. Just like the small hunks of gold that did not measure up, our relationship will never, either.

"Graham, it was fun while it lasted, but you knew it would come to this." I will not allow my emotions to cloud my senses any longer.

"I am tired of trying to convince you we are good together." He finally looks away, sighing and shaking his head.

"I never asked you to save us. You just did."

"And I would do it again, but now you need to save yourself from this place." Then, he places his brown hat on his head and tips it to me in his final farewell.

From the doorframe, I watch Tommy and Graham ride off, realizing this is likely the last time I'm going to see Graham for months. Tommy will take over the route from the town to us, continuing our previous business agreement, but that's all it will be. The thought sinks heavily onto my carved-out chest.

Maggie's arm drapes over my shoulder, and she tries to pull me in. I don't want to be touched and especially not with compassion. I shrug her off and shoulder my way into my jacket. I need to get away.

The smooth burn of brown liquid beckons me with the promise of easing the gaping hole in my chest. My heart is gone. It has ridden off into the night. I didn't want it anymore anyway. My heart has left me weak and exposed, and it won't happen again.

CHAPTER 17

"Another," I say with a harsh bite to the barkeep. His judging brows lift as he polishes a glass, cleaning it thoroughly as he side-eyes me.

My irritation rises as he finishes his task before pouring another shot of whiskey. It will numb the pain and quiet the mind. I need to get away from myself. I intended to avoid this place entirely today, but the more I try to forget what happened two weeks ago, the more it haunts me. Besides, I needed a refill. Later, I'll visit the moonshiners so I can avoid this place entirely.

Looking around, I am the only paying patron in here. One old sloppy miner is passed out in a booth drooling. The dinginess paired with the stale smell of spilled liquor reminds me of how pathetic this place and I are, made worse by the mid-morning light. I dismiss it and throw back my third shot. It will keep me warm and focused.

* * *

Hunting and drinking are the only times my mind is occupied enough not to marinate in the agony of my broken heart. Even hunting, the process of it, is no longer enough to pull me out of this pit. The focus that comes just before a kill is a short relief from my mind that taunts me. *Who were you kidding? It was just a fling. He needed more than what you have. It would never have lasted. He would want something you could never be.* A constant loop of every reason why this thing we had was just a joke became incessant like the buzz of a horse fly in my ear.

Providing for my sisters and maintaining our role as peacekeepers are the only things that matter to me now. Keeping one of my daddy's flasks in my left breast pocket helps the most. Reaching to take another quick swig, my fingers graze across the small gold nugget I keep there too. It is a weight, measurement, and reminder of what I am and am not.

Memories of Daddy have softened over time and a sudden pang of guilt shakes me. I kicked him out and now Graham is gone. *Everyone will leave you in the end*, the voice in my head teases.

Not my sisters, though. They are in this with me. We only have each other.

The daylight and the weight of my flask slowly slip away. Enjoying the mental blur, I collect a rabbit from one of my traps and call it good enough. Usually, I would have tried to hunt until I had enough to feed us for supper and would have another excuse to leave the cabin tomorrow. The less time I spend there the better. That cabin with its quiet dinners and mornings has become a reminder of all of the lost happiness. The memory feels like a scab I can't stop picking.

Shaking my head to clear it, I try to focus before I return, needing to hide my buzz from Maggie. Lately, she has been making snide comments about my drinking, and I don't want to hear it.

Walking through the cabin door, Lottie sees me, pushes up from the floor, and then toddles over to me. I drop the bloody rabbit on the wooden planks, forgetting it will make a mess. All my attention is on my baby sister.

Maggie walks over and picks up the rabbit from the floor. Her eyes narrow at the blood that smears the wooden plank flooring and seeps into the grooves.

Avoiding a fight, I lug Lottie on my hip and snatch a kitchen rag to mop up the mess. Dropping the rag on the floor, I use my foot to wipe at the blood stain. The red smears more, and I have to focus on my balance when I reach down to retrieve the rag, still holding on to Lottie.

Maggie steps toward me quicker than I register and snatches Lottie from me. I finish cleaning up, making sure I don't leave anything behind.

Maggie says flatly, "No word from town yet."

I choose not to respond. Lottie runs back up to me, and I tickle her to get a belly laugh.

"I think that we should make a point to go and visit soon," Maggie continues tentatively.

"Hmmm, I suppose we could make a day trip," I say passively.

"I think we owe them more than a day of our time," she retorts back with some air.

"Maggie, we don't owe anyone anything. We have to think about our situation. The leaves are already turning, and you remember how last winter was. We don't have time to spend down there."

I do not want to discuss this again. We have exhausted this topic. Besides by now, Graham will be long gone on the trading route alone. Who knows if he is still alive? The road is dangerous enough with both him and his father together, but alone he's a sitting duck. Before, when I knew Graham as a kid, these stories excited me, but now they send a pulse of terror through me.

My worry then dances to our precarious situation. Winter preparations are heavy on my mind lately. I'm determined to be fully stocked and ready. We won't need to be saved ever again. I will make sure of that.

Everyone on the mountain is busy getting ready this time but will still turn to us for the basics. I'm not about to worry about another winter where desperation will lead to drastic measures like last year.

"Ellie, I think you should go to Graham. I've been thinking..."

"Maybe you should stop doing that thinking bit." Placing Lottie down on the floor and standing up, I try to get as big as I can to dominate and squash this once and for all.

I continue, "I will not stand for my sisters to be labeled as harlots, which is what those snobby bitches in town will call you. They already look down their noses at us. You and Lottie staying there and me running off to chase after Graham. Ha! We would be the talk of the town. I will not have it. Maggie, you have a chance to marry and have a family of your own. You need to keep your honor and virtue. It's all you have left."

"I think that went out the door once we let Daniel and Graham stay here," she says quietly.

"No, the rumors are about me, not you. I've made sure of that. I won't let you throw your life away for me to go chasing after a man. That will never happen."

"Ellie, what if I told you I didn't want to live up here anymore? I never wanted to live out here. It's just where I was born. We inherited this mess. What if I don't want this anymore?" Maggie replies with a little more confidence and urgency.

"I don't see you living up here forever, either, but you will find a man who will marry you, and then you can go. You are the only one left with a way out, and I will not see you throw it away just because you are desperate to leave here." Frustration starts to take hold of me. Why doesn't she see what this would do to her?

"Ellie, do you hear yourself? Do you want to be here or not?" she asks pointedly.

"What kind of a question is that?" This is all that I am. It's the only home I know. Where else would I go?

"You act as if you want me out but you wouldn't leave, too?"

"There is no leaving for me. I wouldn't fit in anywhere but here. Besides, I have the shop to keep up. You know how it was before Momma and Daddy started it. All the shootings and killings that happened. This place is the only thing keeping those times from happening again. I have no other choice. This is my choice."

Maggie tries a different tactic. "You hate the shop. You always have. If I leave, what will you do?" Maggie brings up a point I have pushed to the side for now.

"I will go on hating it while doing my part. Liking it has nothing to do with it. We don't get the luxury of thinking about whether we like it or not. We are women. We don't get that kind of freedom."

Pain etches Maggie's face as the harsh truth sinks in.

I want to twist the knife. "And you would be good to remember that when looking for a suitor. All you know is how to keep a shop, cook, and clean for God's sake. Pick a guy already so you can get away like you want to."

We both know we're already considered old for marriage; this fact has been on Maggie's mind for a while, so I use it as additional ammo.

Maggie's light blue eyes glisten. "You sound just like him. You smell like him, too."

Wounded, I spin around. *I don't need this shit from her. I'm doing all of this for her and Lottie, and this is the thanks I'm getting?* I've had enough.

As I grab for my coat, I hear the sneer in her voice, "Yeah, I know where you're going. Like that ever helped anything."

"It helps me forget the sad, pathetic life I have here with you." I leave the cabin then and have no intention of returning anytime soon.

Fuming and stomping, my feet carry me to Gunpowder. Nostrils flaring, he nays angrily at me in irritation. I already covered him for the night and settled in.

"Don't *you* start with me," I bite.

Taking off, I direct us to the saloon. It's Saturday night. There will be live music, dancing, and distractions. My mind is now my least favorite place to be.

As mean as I was to Maggie, it was no comparison to the loathing I now feel for myself and how much I'm beginning to sound and act just like *him*.

CHAPTER 18

Maggie is banging around the kitchen; it feels like she's using our cast iron pan on my oversized head. The sun streams in, searing my eyes and taunting me, snidely letting me know how much of the day I have already wasted. I must've missed breakfast again, but why is she making so much noise? I don't know or care, really. It isn't until I hear the second and lower voice drifting from the kitchen that my senses catch up.

My heart quickens at the familiarity and casual cadence in Maggie's voice, and I wonder who it might be. An image of Graham flashes across my anxious mind before I can shut it out. My stomach flips and flutters at the possibility of it being him on the other side of my door. Knowing how I feel would mirror how I must look, I rake my fingers through my hair. Quickly wiping away the sleep and pinching my cheeks, I reconcile that this is as good as it is going to get.

The male voice is low so I still can't decipher who it is. Inhaling deeply, I push through the door into the main room. I register that the man I see before me is scrawny, sweet Tommy. I try not to let the simultaneous relief and disappointment drop in my face appear too obvious. My stomach settles, I square my shoulders and set my efforts to make coffee.

"Tommy, how's it going?" I'm hoping he will offer a word on the one thing I don't want to ask.

"That's why I am up here. Daniel has taken a turn for the worse. Infection has set in." He shifts from one foot to the other, his nerves always so obvious.

Turning around to face him, I register Maggie's travel sacks on the dining table.

Maggie's eyes lock with mine. "Daniel has called for me. He wants us to come and be with him."

"What about Graham?" I try to sound uninterested.

"He isn't back yet, and Daniel didn't want to distract him," Tommy interjects, giving me the facts and then deciding to elaborate. "Graham sent word he has not run into any trouble on the road."

"Yet," I mumble.

Wincing, Tommy turns to Maggie. "Miss Maggie, when would you like to go?"

"*Go?*" My alarm blasts through my response.

"Yes, we are going." Maggie motions to Lottie asleep on the sofa.

"Right now?" Desperation drips from my words as I frantically search Maggie's eyes for clarification.

"Right now, Ellie. We are leaving right now. Are you coming with us?" Her stance is more set than I've ever seen it.

I can't deal with this. My head is pounding, and the brain fog and the buzz cloud the moment. I need time to think.

"How long are you planning on visiting?" Finally, I respond. I need more information.

Maggie stares at me. "It's not a visit. We are not coming back."

"Maggie, be serious." My anxious eyes try to move her.

Tommy chimed in then, "Miss Ellie, Daniel may not make it longer than a week. I'm not sure anyone would mind if they think Miss Maggie is nursing him."

"Shut the fuck up, Tommy," I growl.

"Don't you bite at him, Ellie. This is my choice. Mine." Maggie starts stuffing more of Lottie's clothes into a sack.

"Maggie, are you even thinking?"

"This is the clearest decision I have ever made. Lottie and I are not meant for this life out here. I need to do what's best for her—for us all." She is not budging. "You need to go, too. Go after him. You know that's what you really want."

"All I want is for my sisters to be safe, in our home, where we grew up. I know last winter was bad, but we can do this. Maggie, stay." My voice starts to crack.

"El, give it up. This was not our dream to live out here. It was theirs." She sighs, pointing to my parents' empty room. "And even *they* couldn't make it work. Momma died following Daddy out here, and Daddy stopped living. We can't stop living, and if I stay out here, I will stop living. I choose to live, Ellie."

Pain trickles down my spine, and my hackles go up. "So you haven't been living, huh? All this time up here was just a prison for you?"

Raising her voice to meet mine, she returns, "You could fit in up here. I never did. I never will."

"Momma made you too soft." I aim at what I know will get her. "If she didn't protect you so much, maybe you would see this is our place. There is no changing it."

"And Daddy made you too hard." The heat on her face radiates into a glare.

"At least he taught me to survive," I spit back.

"At least he paid any attention to you at *all*." Her slender chest rises and falls rapidly.

"Oh, yeah, all the times he hit me, and pushed me, and I nearly froze to death at his hands? Yeah, that was his way of telling me he loved me." I roll my eyes to the ceiling and dismiss it.

"Yeah, Ellie, it was. It was the only way he knew how to show it, and he only showed it to you. He gave *you* the tools to survive out here. He gave *you* choices." Real hurt laces her words.

I hitch in a breath, never having considered that. Shaking my head, I try to focus.

"Maggie, you are not leaving. That is not what we do. We stick together. It is the only thing we have left."

"No, it is the only thing *you* have left. I have a man waiting for me, and he needs me. I will not let pride or what other people say about us stop me from living my life." Her words scrape like gravel on exposed soft flesh, sharp, burning, and deliberate.

"Then you are a fucking fool," I say through my clenched jaw. "If Daniel is as bad as Tommy says, he doesn't have long. What then?" The venom in my voice turns icy and vile.

"Then we will deal with it if that day comes." She sucks in a sob.

"I will not watch you throw away the only card you have left to play. No one will want to marry you after this," I protest, trying to make her understand.

"Daniel will."

"Daniel?" My upper lip curls. From the sounds of Daniel's situation, it's likely fatal. She would be left with nothing and surrounded by townies.

"We are planning on getting married in the spring." Her eyes glisten now.

All that time together *did* mean something. Being so caught up in my own whirlwind with Graham, I must've missed it. I knew they were friendly but I had not picked up on romantic.

"*News to me!*" I belt out. Did *everyone* have plans for the future that I didn't know about? Was telling me so terrible that they would keep it from me until they had no other choice but to tell me?

Memories of my momma walking on eggshells before telling my daddy anything rip across my mind. We all knew his initial response was always anger, and evidently so is mine. This realization slaps me in the face, and I start to see red.

"*Go then!* Someone has to take care of what is ours. Leave it up to me just like you *always* have. And when Daniel dies, and you are the talk of the town, I will be waiting here for an apology."

Softly, Maggie replies, "Ellie, you could have so much more than this if you would just let it in."

Swallowing hard, my mouth goes dry. "Not everyone can live in the clouds. Someone has to stay and defend what is ours." I needed a fucking drink, and I needed out of this place.

Walking over to sleeping Lottie, I inhale her scent. I hug her warm little body and then kiss her on the nose.

Like a dream, my body carries me over to the money tin. I briefly pick it up and then shove it into Maggie's arms.

"Take care of them, Tommy," are the last words I say over my cold and hardened shoulder.

CHAPTER 19

The tinkle of the shop bell is the only sound that motivates me to move. Parting from my bed feels like too much effort most days. I only do it to make a rapid sale and then climb back under the covers to escape again.

Two weeks have passed since everyone left. Rolling over in bed, I lie on my back and my muscles ache from lack of movement.

My stomach growls at me, scorning me for not feeding it since yesterday morning, but I roll back over and ignore it. Mentally, I survey my options for food. I had jerky and oats to eat but neither of those quicker options sounds appetizing. Nothing sounds good anymore. The very thought of eating is too much effort. Hunting is out of the question this time of night and isn't necessary since my mouth is the only one needing feeding now.

That isn't entirely true. Gunpowder needs to be fed, watered, and ridden. Taking care of him is the only thing I have left other than the shop, and I am neglecting even him.

No wonder everyone leaves. This task doesn't take much time, anyway. Even when I stretch it out and brush him extra slowly, I still finish quickly and will be at a loss of what to do next. It leaves me with more time to fill up my day.

Sleep is not coming back to me, so I force myself out of bed. It is after closing time and the night darkens the cabin. Lighting a single candle and pulling Lottie's blanket over my shoulders, I pad to the kitchen to boil water.

Keeping the fire for the stove consistently stoked was Maggie's job, and I can see why. I let it burn out again, which means I'll have to start from scratch. This is enough of a chore; I concede defeat and turn my attention to finding the whiskey bottle instead. The thick clear glass bottle is on the counter, discarded, empty, and turned over. Just like I feel inside.

You deserve this, you know? You push everyone away. You have nothing. You are nothing. My mind tailspins through all the ways I've failed everyone I know and care about. My mind reminds me how this ending was inevitable. Despair and pain seep through my bones and render me useless.

I continue to berate myself as the bell on the door twinkles to life. Automatically, I look up.

"I'm closed for the night," I bark out, hoping my tone will send whoever it is on their heels and away from me. I do not want to deal with anyone.

"Hey, El, just stopping by to say hi." Logan waltzes in alone with no posse flanking him. This is new.

"Oh, hey, Logan. What do you need?"

"Like I said, just coming in to check on you. I haven't seen you around." His chipper cadence is grating at me.

"Yeah, well, I've been busy."

"I can tell." I catch his eyes dart to the dishes scattered and the empty whiskey bottle.

He saunters over to the table and reveals a fresh full bottle of whiskey, the kind I tend to favor.

"You do have some redeeming qualities after all," I admit.

Flashing a devilish smile at me, he finds two glasses and pours a heavy serving for us both.

Raising his glass, he says, "To freedom."

I raise my eyebrow instead, intrigued for the briefest of moments. "To freedom?"

"Yes, freedom. This is the first time in your life you don't have anyone to worry about. That, sweetheart, is true freedom."

Considering this, I skip the cheers and drain it down my throat. I'm annoyed I even asked for clarification as I slide my glass over to him for another.

"I still have this Goddammed shop to take care of." I motion with one dismissing hand to the emptiness and darkness around me, my other hand still holding the blanket close for warmth.

"Aw, sure we gotta have something to fill our days, but your nights seem conveniently open now." He makes a point to catch my eye.

His head swivels around to the quiet and slumbering stove, and then he shivers. Topping off my glass, he leaves to start a fire. Shame and guilt tug at me. Embarrassed at the state of this place, I hurry to stack dishes and light more candles.

"Leave it. Don't clean up on my behalf." He enters with an armful of wood.

Maggie was always the hostess, anyway. I don't know what I am doing, but I grab a few pieces of jerky and biscuits. I throw them on a plate without any presentation and start in on one of the biscuits. The dry stale flavor hits my tongue, ash in my mouth; nothing tastes good anymore.

With expert hands, Logan lights the fire, grabs the bottle, and beckons me over to the sofa to sit closer to it. With my glass in hand and Lottie's baby blanket over my shoulders, I am in my night dress only. I pad over and sit.

"Ellie, you can't keep punishing yourself. People leave. You can't count on them. They ain't one of us." His head tips up and drinks again as if what he said is fact and not just opinion.

Following his lead, I drink, starting with a sip. He reaches over and nudges the bottom of my glass up, encouraging more liquid to spill down my throat.

My eyes peer over the edge of the glass, and I can't help my lips from tipping upward.

"There she is." His eyes flirt with mine, the way they have done so many times over the years.

More drinking and less talking are all I want, anyway. Snatching the bottle from his hands, I skip the glass and drink directly from the bottle. I guzzle it down with greedy deep gulps, keeping my eyes on him the entire time.

His smile is dangerous. I realize this is the first time in several days I am not thinking and just doing.

My attention is only on the bottle then, and I continue to chug.

"Hey, hey, hey, it's my turn." Logan rips the bottle from my hands and selfish lips.

He takes it in his large hand and drinks quickly, I watch as the level of the whiskey drops below halfway. I want it back now. Reaching out my hand, I try and snatch it back.

Turning his head away from me, he quickly swaps it to his other hand and then tilts the bottle at a more aggressive angle as he keeps me away with the other, all while continuing to chug my whiskey.

My competitive nature kicks in and nothing else matters but getting that bottle out of his hands and into mine.

Logan stops drinking but does not offer it back. He shakes it lightly, taunting me, just out of my reach. "Come and get it, Ellie."

Sitting back and tucking my feet under me, I prepare to pounce. "You *will* be giving me that bottle back," I drawl out my threat for emphasis.

"I wouldn't be so sure of it." His cocky arrogance eggs me on.

Springing across the sofa, I use the force of my body to pin him back and reach out for the liquid my lips are craving. The whiskey starts to course through my veins at this moment, warming me as it makes its way through me, giving me life. I want more, now.

Logan's muscled arm tightens around my waist as he pulls me back away from what I want. Using the heel of my hand, I push his head up and away to try and stretch as far as I can to grab the bottle. My fingertips graze the bottom of the bottle just before he flips me on my back, pinning me down with his massive legs.

Not giving up my pursuit, I reach up, grasping harshly for the liquid release, my medicine. I continue to fight my way above my head. He uses his other hand to grab both of my arms and pin them down against me. As he looks at me, I continue to wiggle and buck to try and escape but it's useless under his weight.

Inching his face closer to mine, Logan lowers his voice. "You want this. Don't you?"

The smell of whiskey and burning wood clouds my senses. Slitting my eyes, I murmur, "You know I do."

He lowers the bottle closer, teasing me because I can't move. "I will give it to you. Just open your mouth."

My heart pounds in my chest. Trying to decide if I like this or not, the danger and intensity consume my mind hypnotically.

"Ellie, open your mouth." He smiles like a fiend.

Desire, intrigue, and frustration all collide inside of me. The confusion and chaos of it all are so deliciously distracting I savor it.

Logan lowers the bottle close enough I can smell it. Ever so slightly, my lips part. He uses the smooth edge of the bottle opening to trace my lips. Slowly I trace my tongue where the bottle had been and taste the syrupy sweet whiskey on the tip. Logan is watching my every move.

I open my mouth wider, and he takes the invitation, pouring the whiskey in. It saturates my throat as I swallow quickly, greedily.

Pausing he asks, "You want more. Don't you, Ellie?"

Searing him with the challenge in my eyes. I purse my lips and nod once.

So painfully slowly, he lowers the bottle back to my waiting mouth and pours more in, just enough to almost spill over. Gulping it down and nearly choking, I savor the burn it elicits. Enough danger to distract me completely. It's amazing how close pleasure and pain are related.

My vision is starting to get cloudy. The bottle is just about empty.

Logan continues to pin me down and drinks the rest of the whiskey right in front of me.

I watch as the last gulp enters his mouth. I am offended and pissed that he didn't save the last drink for me. But then he stops swallowing mid-drink. Before I can respond, his mouth crushes against mine and he pushes in the last ounce of whiskey into my appalled mouth as his tongue follows.

My body responds to his mouth the same way it had to the whiskey. The blur and escape mimic the effect the alcohol is having on my system.

Logan still doesn't let me go and the restriction ignites my core. Lifting my hips to meet his, I need more friction.

He pulls his face away from mine and asks the same question yet again, "Ellie, you want more. Don't you?"

It's all I want. I want to escape, to forget, to exist—to feel something other than pain and hurt.

"Yes," my voice gravels out from the liquor and lust.

Finally, he releases my arms and legs. We both attack, launching our bodies at each other. Years of want and desire from him and desperation and need from me have us both ripping off clothes and scraping at bare skin. He is rough and rushed, exactly what I need and crave now.

Pulling my nightdress over my head but not off my arms restricts my movement again. My breasts are exposed and lifted for him to instantly devour. Logan lands back on me, leaving my bloomers in place. He arches my low back with one hand and reaches down to the soft fabric separating us with the other. Ripping the delicate fabric easily, he then slams himself into me. A scream escapes my mouth, and I meet his rapid rhythm. My eyes open, and clarity flashes across my mind—not here.

I wrap my legs around his waist as he continues to move and bite at my neck. I demand, "Take me to the kitchen."

Logan follows my command and lifts us both, carrying us still connected to the kitchen table. I discard my nightgown and wrap my arms around his neck. Throwing the chair out of the way, he drops me onto the table top and continues to thrust. I absorb and meet his aggression as we push together. We are both sweaty and ravenous.

"You belong with me. You know that, right?" Logan's deep dominating voice booms out. "You want this. You need this. I want you to come." His order drives me dangerously close to the edge.

My breath pants and grunts out of me.

He's thrusting hard with each word. "Come for me, Ellie. Come for me *now*." He growls out, low, demanding, intoxicating.

I came undone, and oblivion is blissful and violent.

Hearing Logan's deep groan is the only thing bringing me back to reality.

Splayed out on the kitchen table, I allow myself to lie there for a bit longer, savoring the roughness of the table against my exposed skin and what has just happened.

Logan lays his body down on top of mine as our breathing slows down.

"Let's go get more to drink." I want to ride this out for as long as I can. I know once the liquor clears, the reality of what I just did will set in.

Logan gets up and pushes away. "That's my girl."

My girl? "I'm not your girl, Logan. I am nobody's girl. You hear me?" Rushing to my clothes, I start to slide into my nightgown.

I can feel Logan's presence close in on me. He wraps his arms around me from behind and starts to lick the back of my neck.

"This is how it is supposed to be," he whispers into my ear.

Even through the haze of my buzz, something inside of me is sad and bruised.

"You are one of us. You need to be with one of your kind." He lifts the soft garment I had just replaced up enough to snake his hand under the hem and then grazes the sensitive tissue just under my breast, not touching or grasping, yet.

"This is you. You are wild. I want you wild." His hand finally goes where I primally want it to. He kneads one breast for distraction, while the other makes its way between my legs.

Logan is right. This is who I am. It's what I have always been.

Love and fairy tales of marriage are for women like Maggie. Why I had thought it could be any other way for me was all just an illusion, a dream meant for softer girls. It was never meant to come true. I would never love Logan, and that was better, safer for me. He'll be my distraction, and that is the best I can hope for.

"I see it in you, El. We can be that for each other." His unspoken words say to me, *It takes one to know one.*

"Fuck it." I rip off my gown and allow him to consume me.

CHAPTER 20

Losing hours on end is a violent reprieve. I will pay for it later, but for now, I savor the slide into oblivion as it pulls me under each time. Chasing away the present moment with more whiskey helps. The alcohol illness in the mornings gives me another excuse to drink even more. It is the only remedy I have other than Logan. Hits come in the forms of sex, liquor, and blackness.

Days blur and slur into nights after the first night together. Scraps and shreds of images rip across the fleeting moments of consciousness. Logan and I tangled together, dancing on tables, poker games lost and won, shootouts turned dangerous because neither of us could see straight, and horse races through other people's lands consume me. These moments focus and fade quickly. Did all that really happen?

Logan and I never end up in bed together or on the sofa. Only hard and exposed places would get me there now. We aren't officially together but we're never apart.

My refusal to *be* Logan's is starting to anger him. Yet, he's still enjoying the chase. I have to admit he's helped me out of the broken shattered place I had been festering in. His distraction has given me the energy to harden and numb myself into a safe bunker.

Tonight, we plan to head out toward the bootleggers' camp to stock up on some moonshine for the week. Whenever we're kicked out of the saloon, we need supplies for after. Hearing the multiple hooves approach, I shove my full flask into my breast pocket. Spending so much time with Logan means I'm also around Tricia and the whole Clancy Gang.

Checking the mirror, I see my hair is loose and sticking out all over. Dark circles cradle my vacant eyes. I look as good as I feel, *like shit*, but I could care less. I use the mirror as another way to remind me of the life I now lead and no longer a tool for fixing or refining anything.

I lock up quickly, closing the door before they can dismount.

"Whoa, you look like absolute horse shit," Tricia repeats the words I had just used to describe myself.

"Fuck you, too," I reply to her in greeting.

Logan just chuckles. "We gotta do an errand before we head out to the still."

I don't respond. Errands for these guys usually mean trouble.

"I'll just meet you out there," I try to hedge.

"It's on the way. It won't take long," Logan dismisses.

"What is it then?" I want to know what I am getting into.

Getting closer, he lowers his voice in a tone as if I owe him something. "Aww, it's nothing. Just collecting on a payment. I could use an extra hand, El."

This request echoes the one his daddy asked of mine all those years ago, and it shakes me to the core. Up until now, I have been able to just party and play with Logan, but lately, it feels as if he wants more than just a playmate. He wants a partner in crime—to have me as one of them, truly and ultimately.

Tension and laughter spread across the others flanking Logan. My guts tighten in on me. Making a point to stay out of this part of Logan's business is getting harder the more I spend time with them. Yet their chaos distracts me from my own misery, which keeps me coming back.

Logan trots his horse over. "It's nothing. Someone owes me money. He has it now. We'll collect it and then be done." He's trying to reassure me.

"What, Ellie. Are you scared?" Tricia sneers and taunts me.

Pulling myself onto Gunpowder, I take off after Logan and make a point to kick the dust back at her painted face. The rest of them follow.

Our horses gallop on the dirt road, in a line, to the mountain valley.

Logan shouts over his shoulder, "I bet I'll beat all you sorry sons of bitches to the river."

No one verbally responds. I spur Gunpowder to a sprint.

We are all neck and neck.

The rest of them try to keep up but Logan and I are better riders and easily pull ahead. We push our horses faster, weaving through trees and jumping over logs.

We are equals until the last corner where Gunpowder makes a quicker turn and pulls us ahead. Gunpowder's hooves slosh into the river's edge in victory.

Logan isn't used to being beaten, let alone by a woman, and had always been a sore loser.

His mood shifts from playful to sharp.

"Just like your daddy always said, you were built rough like a man—and you ride like one, too."

The backhanded compliment picks at the scab of a wound that cuts deep. Sarcastic words are something I know and understand, though, so I find some comfort in the consistency of this. It feels familiar so it must be true.

The rest of the gang enters the clearing then.

Logan turns his horse and leaves me behind, not announcing who won. "So here's how it's gonna go. We ride into their camp, and I'll do all the talking."

They all nod as they reach for their guns and then take off. I don't have time to ask questions so I just follow and intentionally fade to the back of the herd.

Logan raises his gun in the air and fires as we approach a miners' encampment. All four miners' heads snap up then they stop what they are doing, frozen in their tracks.

Gunpowder and I gallop up but he stops us earlier than I tell him to. We are both tense, uncomfortable, and alert.

"You remember us?" Logan says, looking down his nose at the grizzled man who appears to be in charge.

"Yes, sir, I remember yeh," he answers shakily.

"It's collection day." Logan circles the man on his horse.

"We paid you last week." The lead miner tries to sound more assertive.

"That was last week. Payday comes around when I say it does." Logan's voice turns to ice. Chuckles from his backup rumble around me

Payday?

One of the other miners takes off away from us and toward his own rifle. He's about a foot away when Logan raises his pistol and shoots the man in the back. The bullet punches him, his arms flail, and he face dives. When he lands, he's dead instantly. Blood spreads in a dark rapid stain across the dingy weathered shirt, saturated in seconds.

My eyes widen as my whole body begins vibrating. Gunpowder steps back, sensing my panic.

Logan slides down off his horse and presses the red-hot barrel of his pistol into the first miner's temple. The miner winces in pain as the heat singes his flesh. Without another word, he hands over all their gold without hesitation.

Logan accepts the bag and tips his hat before climbing back into his saddle.

It's all over before I have time to respond. I'm still at the back of the pack, and my eyes meet with the man who handed over the gold. He surveys my face as I ride by numbly. Turning my head quickly, I race off after the rest of them to avoid recognition, but it's too late.

He saw me, and I know him. He is a patron who comes to our shop often. Usually, he buys dried beans, jerky, and candles. He fancies my sister's cookies, too, and is even wearing one of her gray fur coats. He is a simple miner who only panned for what he needed and had even been a guest over to our house for dinner when my momma was alive.

Numbness, terror, shame, and guilt take over.

We ride to the distillery where a monstrous bonfire is already dancing maliciously into the sky, blazing in a way only pure alcohol can motivate the flames. Watching as everyone leaps off their horses, I remain glued to my saddle. I have gone too far and crossed a line now.

Without a word, I turn to leave.

Deep rapid hooves follow me, and Logan cuts in front of my path. "Where are you goin'?"

"I am goin' home." The reality of the situation settles in.

"But the party is just getting started," he insists, lightening his voice to the playful banter he knows I enjoy.

"Logan, you just shot a man," I snap out.

"Yeah, before he could do the same to any of us."

"Because you backed them into a corner."

"Ellie, he owed me. He'd been skimpin' out on payments. He and his buddies need to know we don't allow it."

The *we* in his sentence unsettles me most.

"I know them. They would have been good for it."

"If you let people off the hook, it'll get around, and then everyone will be expecting leniency." His words echo a similar stance and tone I used with Maggie in the past.

"What did he owe you?" I need to understand.

"His local tax," he replies as he brushes a loose wave of hair from my face.

I shake away from the same hand that pulled the killing trigger. "What tax?"

"The tax all miners have to pay if they don't want any trouble," Logan says as if he were commenting on the weather.

"So basically you're stealing from them?"

"It's not stealing. We offer protection from anyone else in the area who tries the same. But if they don't pay, we don't protect them."

My brows crumple in disgust and anger. I yank on my reins to get around Logan. Just as I am about to work Gunpowder into a gallop, Logan shouts pointedly, "You are a part of it now."

Halting abruptly, I huff, "I had nothing to do with it."

"I didn't see you stopping anything. That makes you part of it."

The realization slaps me in the face. I did nothing. It makes me just as bad as the rest of them.

Logan smiles as he can see the understanding settle into my reaction.

"See, you are one of us now."

Shaking my head, I try to back away.

He continues, "This is complete freedom, Ellie. You were still holding back. I gave you this as a gift. Now *we* are unstoppable." There he is again, using *we*.

How have I ended up here? How have I fallen so far?

He offers up a small jar of moonshine.

More words of hate fling through my mind. *You are one of them. You deserve this. There is no going back now. It was inevitable. This is all you have left.*

Snatching the clear jar, I spin the metal lid off so fast it falls and clinks to the ground. The alcohol smell knocks me in the face. The hot and toxic liquid burns my throat as I swallow it down along with the last of my belief that I am any different from these people. I'm conceding that I deserve this.

ONE DAY AT A TIME

CHAPTER 21

The thick heat from the room hits my face first. A freshly stoked fireplace laced with velvety smoke and pine sap fills my nostrils. I have not started a fire or chopped wood lately, however.

Shit, winter is coming and by now I should have had all my fuel fallen, chopped, and stacked. Another fail. Dismissing this, I try to orient myself.

My whole body is warm, almost too hot, except for my toes. They're still sore from being cold. My eyes slit open but my neck is too weak to lift. Scanning the room, I don't recognize where I am. The cabin is small and simple; it had a warmth about it that is not just coming from the crackling fireplace in the corner but also from the feminine touches scattered around the room.

The rustic flower arrangement is made with interesting, gnarled twigs, grasses, and red wildflowers on the simple dining table and handmade quilted throw blankets are scattered around. Strength and beauty have been weaved within them.

I notice the gray wolf sleeping next to the fire and connect with where I must be. But how the hell did I get here?

I roll on my back, and my head feels two sizes too big. This small movement causes my vision to blur, slanting and spinning me while I remain still. My stomach flips so I lean over and decide to retch on the floor. I realize a gray metal pan sits conveniently next to me. It catches the acid from my mouth; I didn't have anything left in my belly so it burns me as it exits my mouth. I can't remember the last time I ate. My throat is sore, so this vomit is not the first to leave my body today.

Wiping my lips, I sit up. Fin, the gray wolf, lifts his oversized head and looks at me with yellow golden eyes. I hear his owner working in the kitchen. The flap of her pet's tail has her looking up and then shaking her head.

Looking down at the floor, I am not ready to confront why I ended up on her sofa and in her cabin. I am afraid to know what happened. *How the fuck did I get here?*

The last thing I remember, we were pressing a herd of cattle down a dangerous mountain face. They were not ours. I can still smell the singe of burning cowhide. Then I lost time, maybe hours until I hazily recall an image of me on a tabletop, my skirts hiked way too high up on my thighs, then nothing. Blackouts happen to me almost every night now.

Aponi comes over to me with a steaming cup of tea, offering it over with her wrinkled but strong leathered hands. "Drink this, and slowly." Her gray and black hair frames her face while the rest, in a loosely braided rope, ends mid-way down her spine.

Sipping, I taste willow bark, peppermint, and some citrus. The fluid hits my empty stomach hard, so I just cradle the cup in my hands. Fin's tail starts to thump against the worn wooden floor panels as Aponi comes closer, and she takes a moment to pat him on the head. She then approaches me again and bends down to fetch the soiled pan.

Looking at me pointedly, she asks, "Do I have time to clean this out?"

I nod, though I am risking losing my guts even now. I will hold it just to prove I can.

She brings the clean pan back swiftly and sits in the wooden rocking chair across the room from me. A colorful purple quilt is draped over the back of the thick solid arch supporting her spine. It is positioned next to the fire and Fin's bed. Fin nestles in closer to her feet.

She sits back, and her wrinkled beautiful face takes me in. Unease fills my chest as her too-attentive eyes scrutinize me.

"You are looking better now. I thought you might've been out there too long and some of those toes might need lopping off," she huffs.

My eyes widen as I clumsily inspect my exposed toes. They have a slight bluish hue to them but the color appears rapidly when I press the skin. Blood is still flowing; I sigh in relief.

"Where'd you find me?" I mumble out. A mixture of wanting to know and not wanting to know ripples through me. My own version of self-flagellation.

"You were outside, exposed in the cold, wearing that ridiculous dress without a coat. I found you around the back of the saloon, or more, Fin found you. You're lucky he likes whiskey as much as you do." Fin's tail wags in agreement or because his master said his name. Either way, it feels like he is mocking me too.

"Your dog drinks whiskey?" I ask.

"Only when he is a very good boy or if it is a special occasion." Aponi admires Fin, scratching the thick gray fur behind his ears. His tail thumps a few more times.

"Was I out there alone?" I'm feeling out just how bad I must've been last night.

"Yeah, I think your drinking buddies forgot you there. Not that I would call them buddies if they left you as they did in the state I found you. Some friends *you* have."

"Yeah, well, we tend to take care of ourselves. If someone can't keep up, then that's their own problem," I say dismissively.

Lately, I have been wandering off, I admit to myself. Usually, I would wake up on my way back to our cabin. Once, I even woke up on the ground next to Gunpowder. He grazed on some fresh grass and waited for me to become conscious enough to take us home. Even the look in his big black eyes appeared disappointed. His temperament changed toward me after that night.

Aponi's structured, angled black brows furrow, scowling at me. "I would say that a fair statement in general, but when someone isn't able to walk or figure their way home, you would think those people you spend so much time with would look after you a bit?"

I don't want to process this and don't really care about anything other than my splitting head and getting home. I didn't want help from her or anyone else. Even if that meant I am discarded alone to freeze.

"Well, I appreciate you taking care of me but I should be going now." Setting the tea down, I rise up, but the room tosses and bucks wildly so I plunk my butt back down on the buttery soft brown leather sofa. I reach for the pan just in case.

"As I figured, you're still wasted. You stay put until the spins stop rattling that head of yours." She seems to dismiss that I need any more convincing seeing as I could not even stand. She turns to open up the stove to throw another rough cut of pine into the already blazing fire.

I watch as she tends to the flames with fluid motions. I have seen Aponi here and there. In the woods, panning for gold, in the store; she always holds her head up high with an almost arrogant air. Yet now that I am closer and can observe her more directly, I see she is calmer and more confident. She moves with ease—a certain poise that is unlike most mountain dwellers.

She is respected and revered by all. No one messes with her—not out here or in town. Yet she is always alone apart from Fin who never leaves her side. She seems just so... I don't know, comfortable in her skin, something I know nothing about. She is so out of the ordinary in the way she holds herself as if it defines her.

She looks over her shoulder and reminds me to drink up. I sip tentatively on the warm concoction in my trembling hands. I know it's supposed to help with this damn hangover so I force myself to drink bigger gulps, attempting to dilute the brown liquid that is still at a steady state in my bloodstream.

"Ellie, you are in that bar more and more—almost as much as your pa was before he took off. What are you doing spending all your time in that place? Don't you have a family to feed?" Her direct questions catch me off guard.

Peering up from the mug, only looking a little ahead of me to avoid eye contact, I reply, "They're gone. They don't need me anymore. Didn't you hear? Maggie went to be with Mr. Parson. She took Lottie with her too. Everyone must be talking about it. Oh, the scandal." Sarcasm masks my anger and flicks from my tongue easily now.

Aponi nods. "I see. Well, what about Graham? I know you two were close for a while."

"Graham is gone too," I bite out through tight lips.

Aponi seems to note the tension in my voice. "Well, that's a shame. You two seemed to have an easy way about you."

I just don't have the energy to respond. How did I get here? How did even Aponi know about this? How am I waking up in this woman's cabin? How had I gotten to this place where I wouldn't, no *couldn't* make it home? Everyone I cared about is gone and here I am unable to stand, let alone walk home. *Fucking useless.*

"Thank you for taking me in. I'm sorry if I inconvenienced you in any—" I start to say but then Aponi cuts me off.

"Now, none of that. I did what you would have done for me had you stumbled across my drunken ass." She sits back down in her chair and settles in. The clip of her words has me following her direction without question—almost as if she knows I'll respond better to them in this way.

I want to get out of there, to lick my wounds in solitude and crawl into bed and never come out. But it's not a choice for me currently, so I lie back down.

Aponi's piercing golden-brown eyes rest on me, observing me and taking in all my wasted splendor. I am feeling sorry for myself. *How pathetic have I really become?* I raise my arm over my eyes to shield them from the light and from her.

Drifting back to sleep is the only escape I have available to me at this moment, so I slow my breath to force myself into unconsciousness.

* * *

Clinking in the kitchen wakes me up. I'm not sure how long I was out again but the sun is coming up. I sit up this time with more confidence, and the room does not turn on me.

Aponi is in the kitchen, and I smell the fat from the bacon mixing with the smell of buttery biscuits. Walking to the kitchen, I sit down at the table. I am still a shoeless heathen; I can't find my boots or stockings.

The table is small, and I take the one chair closest to me, leaving the only other chair for Aponi. Fin trots over to me. He is tall enough to sit back on his haunches and his large head comes up to my belted waist. I pat between his eyes at first, petting where a white patch rests, but then he unexpectedly puts the full weight of his head in my lap. I absorb this contact in a way that is more comforting to me than to him.

Aponi puts coffee in front of me and looks at me with a softer smile. "There you are." She places the warm biscuits in front of me.

She then snaps and motions her finger over to Fin's bed by the fire, and her companion obeys without hesitation. He plops his heavy body down and curls up into a gray roll. Aponi's wolf is not allowed to beg, I guess.

Aponi brings over the rest of the breakfast and encourages me to dish it up. I fill my plate with bacon, two biscuits, and two eggs. My stomach feels ready for this but my head is still tight.

We start to eat, and I can feel the strength seeping back into my body with each bite of nourishment and fat. I drink all of the coffee in my mug, and she pours me another. She also places water in front of me and nudges it closer to me. I chug it down and turn back to the coffee.

"So, what are you going to do now?" Aponi asks me bluntly.

"What do you mean?" Is she talking about after breakfast?

"Well, now that your ma, pa, sisters, and Graham are all gone, what are you going to do now?"

I shrug my shoulders. "I have the shop to keep. Hunting and panning for gold—what else is there to do?"

She looks me straight in the eyes and says, "Yeah, that's what I'm asking you. Now that you don't have all those people to worry about, what are you going to do?"

I am confused. "I have to take care of the store. That's what I am *supposed* to do." I'm repeating myself again. Either she is dense or I am slower from the residual alcohol in my system.

Aponi returns, "Says who?"

Again, I am not understanding her. "It's just what we do. We hunt, stock supplies, and pan for gold. What else is there? We are the peacekeepers. Now it is up to me." There is no more *we*. I gotta stop using that word.

Aponi sits back in her chair. "Well, there is a lot you could do. You could go to town with your sisters, you could catch back up with Graham, you could just hunt to feed yourself, you could gold pan full time, you could keep the shop going, or close it. From my point of view, you could do anything you want now that you don't have to do anything at all."

I set my fork down and look at her warily. "Yeah, well, it's all I know how to do. 'ides, you remember how it was before. That shop is the main thing keeping the peace. It's more important than ever since my sisters are in town," I try and rationalize to this odd old woman.

"Oh, so you like to take care of the shop then?"

"I mean, it isn't a matter of liking it or not. It's what I need to do."

"Says who?"

I can feel the heat rise in my chest. "No one has to *say* it. It's just what I am supposed to do. Without me, there would be riots in the street and killings again."

Not to mention my parents' legacy, the only thing we have of them, would be lost. If I wasn't there to defend it, someone could claim it for their own. In fact, I wonder, is that what this old woman is feeling me out for? My defenses are back in action. *Tread lightly now, Ellie.*

Aponi replies confidently, "There haven't been those types of killings in over fifteen years, so maybe it is time to see how it goes."

I slam my coffee mug down. "*See* how it goes? Why don't we just let all those roughnecks around those townies and see how it goes? Yeah, that sounds smart."

"Well, eventually, that's going to happen anyway. You can't live forever," Aponi says bluntly.

"By then, my sisters and I will be dead so it won't matter to me anymore."

"Ah, so it's still your sisters you are trying to protect, huh? So they chose to leave you but you have to stay to keep all the harm and wildness away. Is that right?"

"That's right."

"So, no harm can come to them in town? No illness, or accident, or passing-through outlaws—nothing like that can happen?"

I widen my eyes. "Well, yes, I suppose. But at least I can control the line and keep it as far from them as possible," I respond confidently with a hint of righteous indignation. What else is there?

Aponi goes to clear the table so I stand to help her. She eyes me, and I sit back down.

Picking up my coffee, I drain the rest of it down. I am done with this conversation. I am ready to turn it on her. If she can ask me all these personal questions, why can't I?

"Why do you live up here all alone, keeping to yourself? All you have is you and your mutt. You're up here with us roughnecks, yet you act like you are better or somethin'. You go to town and hold your head up high but never interact with anyone. Why do you think you are better than *everyone*?"

I watch her start to clean the dishes. She never breaks from her tasks as she simply replies, "It is all intentional."

Rolling my eyes, I push back away from the table and go to stand.

She continues, "Everything I do I have *chosen* to do in my particular way. I have chosen to live in the mountains because it is where I find the most peace. I have my Fin because I do get lonely sometimes. I do not interact with the roughnecks, as you call them, because it is not the life I want to live or the people I want to spend my time with.

"The townsfolk respect me because I demand it from them. They don't bother me, and I don't bother them. I do not care what they think of me. I had a love and he died, and that was all there was for me. I have always been an outcast since my mother was Native American and my father was white. Everything I do I have consciously chosen, so I am at peace with my life. Can you say that for yourself?"

The honesty, bluntness, and question blindside me. I don't know what to say. She is challenging my very way of life. Accusing me that I have a choice to live differently. As if I *chose* this loneliness. It was not a choice. It was given to me. I have no choice. This is my life. These are the cards I was dealt. All she does is worry about herself. I had to worry about *everything and everybody.*

My hackles come up. "You don't know me or what I have gone through!" My heart is pounding, and my head is still dizzy from last night.

Who is she to talk to me like this? We have never talked for more than a couple of words in all these years and she is questioning me like this? I am done here.

I stand up and stalk to the door. "Thank you for taking me in. It won't happen again."

Locating my worn brown leather boots by the door, I tug them on. Noticing the vomit on the tip of one only pisses me off more. I slam the door behind me. The morning air nips at my exposed shoulders as I start the trek home. I must've lost my coat last night, so I only have the low square neckline of my bodice from the simple yet feminine drapes of my sister Maggie's forgotten dresses. The one was dark blue with a white ruffled bodice; she had originally made it for me but I never wore it until now.

My mind is spinning, and the heat in my chest burns hotter. I'm not cold; I'm just fucking pissed.

Fuming and ruminating, I think, *She doesn't know me and doesn't know all I'm responsible for. She is the outcast and by choice? Ha! They all left me. It makes sense, though. Look at me. I can't even take care of myself let alone my family. No wonder why they all deserted me.*

Gah! I am just so fucking tired. I want to escape the deafening whirlwind tunnel gusting about the vise grip that is my head. I need a fucking drink.

Finally, I make it back to my cabin. Throwing on one of Maggie's thick, brown, wolf-hide fur coats for immediate warmth, I aptly build an angry fire and stand next to it as it comes alive.

Setting the kettle on the fire, I wait for the water to boil. I know I don't have any liquor here. I would have to make the trip back out to the bootleggers' camp or the saloon, and I do not want to deal with that ridicule.

Deciding more sleep would be best for me, I leave Maggie's coat on. Grabbing for the throw blanket and forcefully dragging the sofa closer to the fireplace, I settle in, lying on my side.

The fire in my belly is hard to keep roaring with how cold and alone I feel. I consider Aponi's question and wonder *what if?*

What if I don't have to take care of the shop? What if I *did* leave? What if I could be with Graham? *What if?* The thoughts are so foreign yet peaceful to me that they take me to a place of restful sleep, unlike any sleep I have had for a long time.

CHAPTER 22

An aggressive thick fist banging on the door wakes me up. My head pounds in a steady beat as my eyes open. The light from the mid-morning sun streams in from the window directly across my face. This means it must be past nine. I should've had the shop ready and open for over an hour. I never had to worry about this when Maggie was here. *This isn't my job, anyway,* I curse. *It is now.*

Shooting up from the sofa and rushing for the latch, I unlock and open it up much faster than I intend to. Logan's broad antagonizing smile and the sun silhouetting his head sear my eyes.

"It's just you," I mumble out.

"Ellie!" he says too loudly on purpose.

His tromping steps pound into the shop in unison with the drumming beat at my temple. I go behind the counter to start my opening chores. He has a skip in his fucking step, and I hate him for it. He drank more than me, but he never seems to feel the punishment I feel after a night like that. I don't know if I have ever had a night like that. I am regretting everything I do remember and beg to God that Logan doesn't retell those bits my blackout so graciously removed from my memory.

His followers trail behind him. Tricia and the boys smile at me as they crowd the shop's entrance. Tricia seems extra happy today, and I know it is at my expense.

"The great Ellie dancing on the table and shooting bottles off people's heads! I never thought I would see the day you were in a dress doing it all at the same time." Tricia's smile doesn't go to her eyes; her malicious tone pokes at my nerves as she laughs in my face.

"I wouldn't want you to be the only one having all the fun." I use sarcasm to hide my embarrassment.

"Oh, Ellie, Tricia is just jealous you can be that fucked up and still dance better than her." Logan slings his heavy arm over my shoulders as he comes around the corner. He places a big wet sloppy kiss on my cheek.

I try to pull away, not wanting to be touched, but he holds me tighter to his side. He reaches into his pocket and pulls out a pint-sized bottle of my favorite whiskey before swiftly handing it to me. Thankfully, he's not teasing me with it.

"I thought you might need this today, honey." Logan smiles at me. He knows I'm in pain.

Holding the bottle in my hand gives me a sense of relief as I knew it would. It will cure the sickness both physically and mentally. It will stop all the racing thoughts colliding in my head. Not only am I chastising myself for the bullshit show I put on last night, but now I also have Aponi's words confusing me. I need to shut it all off.

Logan nudges the bottle in my hand when the bell on the shop door jingles to life. My eyes widen as Aponi walks in with

Fin trailing her, his tail wagging. She takes in the room, Logan, and the bottle in my hands. She looks at me, her golden-brown eyes connecting with mine, seeing me deeply. I want to run.

Logan releases me and saunters around the counter. He leans against it while the other three observe the shop's contents, pretending to be distracted.

Aponi walks up to the counter next to Logan as if he is not even there. "You're open today."

As if it's not a given, I say, "'Course I am. It's past nine. Isn't it?"

Aponi shrugs and says, "I guess. But after the night you had, I thought maybe you'd take it easy today."

Logan laughs out loud. "That's not what Ellie does. She gets back to it. She ain't no lightweight freeloader. She knows how to saddle back up and ride hard." Aponi does not miss his insinuation.

My cheeks heat and I glare at Logan. He shrugs and then looks away.

Aponi squares right up, toe to toe with Logan. "If you were any sort of a respectable man, you wouldn't talk to her like that. Or leave her alone passed out behind the tavern."

She sounds more like a mother than another mountain-dweller, and again this catches me off guard. People stick to their own business out here. Sticking out your neck may cost you your throat. The Aponi I thought I knew keeps to herself and never gets in the middle of things like this.

Tricia's voice cuts out from the corner, "Ooooh, the ol' lady is scolding you, Logan. You gonna let her talk to you like that?" The other two snicker behind her.

Logan stands taller and uses his whole body to take up more space. He looks down his nose at her with venom in his eyes. "You think Ellie doesn't like all this? She *is* this. You don't know a thing about it."

"And you do?" Aponi challenges.

Logan steps up to Aponi, and Fin's hackles bristle. The wolf's deep growl rumbles across the room. One motion from Aponi and her beast would strike.

Logan seems to realize this, so he moves a hand to his pistol and steps back. His cool demeanor returns.

He is still looking at Aponi as he says, "Ellie, we are going to go out tonight. Fire at the falls. There's a new batch of moonshine they want us to taste. Want to ride out there together?"

My head bobs in unconscious acceptance. Pushing up from the counter, Logan leaves the liquor behind. He smiles directly at Aponi without breaking eye contact. He struts out like he won some unspoken game, and the rest of them trail behind him as they leave.

Tricia turns her head over her dainty shoulder, cloaked in one of Logan's coats, "Oh, and Ellie, maybe wear pants tonight instead of that dress. You don't know how to wear one, anyway. 'sides, you wouldn't want anyone else to see that white ass of yours again." They all bust up and laugh hysterically as my stomach drops to the floor. Last night was *bad*.

My hand flies to the bottle in front of me. Aponi eyes the bottle and then me. I release it from my death grip and realize just how tightly I've been squeezing it.

Aponi steps away to scan the shop's products. She decides on a bag of rice, some beans, and a few potatoes. I stay quiet and busy myself with stoking the fire.

"Do you want some coffee or tea?" I ask her tentatively, ducking my head from her to avoid eye contact. I am not sure why but I shy away from her.

"Do you actually want my company or are you just askin' to be polite?" she fires back, still turned away from me she inspects one of my sister's coats for sale.

This stops me in my tracks. What? What the hell does she mean? I remember my mother's patience with people in the shop and try to channel her at this moment. Warily I think, *What am I supposed to say?*

If I'm being honest with myself, I'm not sure if I want her to stay. On one side, her questions from last night and this morning are still whirling around in my head. Then there is this involvement in my life over the last twenty-four hours, which I still don't understand. I feel like I owe her now, and I don't like owing anyone. But the shame from last night is crippling, and if she left then I could easily drown it away.

I still had no answer for her.

"Girl, what are you thinking?" She stops shopping and looks straight at me.

This is the first time I have ever been asked what I am thinking, and for some reason, I want to tell her the truth. So I do.

"I am embarrassed about last night, and I am sorry you had to deal with it all. I don't honestly know if I want you to stay or go. Part of me wants you here because I can't stop thinking about this morning and another part of me wants you to go so I can forget this ever happened." My heart pounds, and I hitch back at my own honesty.

She does not smile but the light in her eyes connects with mine. "I think this is the first real conversation you've had in a long time. Am I right?"

I just stare, stuck in my spot. I am not sure I have ever been this honest about what I'm thinking to anyone. Even Graham. Sure, he had a way of getting me out of my head, but I would never let him into the whirlwind of chaos that takes up residence permanently there. I have never truly let my guard down around anyone.

With her callused hard finger, she motions for me to sit on the sofa. She takes the rough wood from my hand and tends to the fire. Fin sits next to me on the wood floor, his body warming my feet.

"Ellie, why did you open your store today?"

"Because it's my job to be open. It's what I do," I say matter-of-factly, echoing the words I had told her in her cabin this morning. Why is she not getting this—my importance, my role, my place?

"Says who?" she asks me this incessant question yet again.

"Why do you keep asking me that?" I blow out a breath and slump down in my seat impatiently.

"Because, girl, I want you to think. Who's keeping you here? Who is demanding you carry on like this?" She grabs a chair from the dining table and pulls it closer to the fire.

Crossing my arms and squirming in my seat, I answer curtly, "Momma and Daddy set this place up for us. It was their dream to be here. They built something for us out of nothing. Now it's my job to keep it safe." I want to explain it all to her so she understands and stops pestering me with all this garbage. "Besides, when they *all* come to their senses and come back, I will be ready."

"What if they never come back?" Aponi poses the question I have dismissed so many times. I'm not ready to accept this.

"Then I will do what is expected of me—keep their legacy alive."

"So *you* are the one saying *you* need to open the shop. To be here, to keep the peace? You are responsible to do all of this alone? I suppose that makes you the boss. Doesn't it?" I watch as Aponi lets those questions hover between us.

"I mean, no one has to say it. It's just what is expected of me. And I suppose it does make me the boss now." *And* the owner. This realization sets me back.

Rapidly answering her questions helps me actually hear my own words as they leave my mouth. On one hand, I am acting like all those people in my life are still here, telling me how to be, how to act, and what to do. But in reality, I am now the shop and landowner. *Can I make the rules now?*

"So what do you want to do, Ellie?" Aponi asks again after allowing me time to process.

I want to be done with this interrogation but I can't unsee what she's just blasted a beam of light on.

No, I can't think this way. What is she trying to do to me? Narrowing my eyes at her, I scream, "This is my job. This is all I know. This is all I am good for. Without this I have nothing. I *am worth nothing!*"

She sits up taller in her chair, the wrinkles on her face highlighted by the glow of the fire. I brace myself for anger and loud words, surveying her to prepare my counterattack. She just stands up.

"There it is. That's what's holding you back. It looks like you are going to have to find another way to feel worthy," she says simply. She has no malice, hidden agenda, or attempt at one-upping me in her face, eyes, or cadence.

She whistles to Fin as she fishes the money out of her pocket to pay me for the items. She turns to leave, but before she closes the door, she turns to me.

"I am gold pannin' tomorrow. You wanna come? I could teach you."

I am still reeling from what I just said. She's acting like I didn't just scream at the top of my lungs, spilling my deepest darkest secret to her—to myself. I want to scoop those words back in and stuff them deep back down inside me where no one, including me, could find them again. It is too late, though. Now I can't run away from it; someone else knows.

She continues when I don't say a word, "I'll be around at sunup. Maybe don't stay up so late tonight." She eyes me one last time and tips her dark brown, cracked leather hat.

My look of disbelief and confusion is painted across my haggard face. Anger and fights were part of what I know; I didn't understand this sort of talk. I am exhausted yet relieved.

"Aponi, I know how to pan for gold. I already do it alone," I reply tiredly.

"I know you do, and it's why I want to take you. You are good at what you do. Everyone knows it. But you still have a lot to learn and I think I can help." Aponi then clicks for Fin to follow. I don't think we're talking about panhandling anymore.

Her penetrating eyes rip down all my shields again so I cross my arms to create space and protection. It's as if I can't shrink away from her. I'm still not sure what she really means by all this, but I'm so blindsided I can't think. It's like no matter my retort, she has a smoother, wiser response. Her grounded confidence shakes me to the core.

"Tomorrow then?" Aponi asks over her shoulder, not waiting for my response before she leaves me there alone.

On the sofa, I am left dumbfounded, still trying to make sense of it all. Scanning the room, I'm not sure what to do next.

What do I want to do? This is the first time ever I consider *my* preference.

All I want is a bath and my bed. I don't want to deal with the shop. I don't want to be open today. *I'm the owner now, damn it.*

My feet carry me to the heavy iron latch, and I bolt it shut. Next, I reach for the hand-painted sign my momma made, and for the first time since it was hung, I flip it to the *closed* side and it remains that way for the rest of the day.

CHAPTER 23

I set my attention to brewing my coffee and take in the silence around me. Filling the kettle, I listen to the water hit the iron. I stoke the fire and hear the crackles, and the water starts to agitate as the temperature rises. The soft coos from the mourning doves outside have me lost in the moment. I pull out the cream *and* sugar this morning, deciding to change up my normal and more practical version of pure blackness.

While sipping on the sweet concoction, I remember how much I love this time of day. When was the last time I noticed all of this? Have I really ever appreciated any of it?

I have given up early mornings since everyone left. Sleeping in reduced the sentence of another lonely fruitless day. I rarely made it home before two a.m. anyway. Last night was no different. Thankfully I am only a little fuzzy this morning.

I snap out of my reverie and make myself a quick breakfast of grits, a fat pork sausage, and two fried eggs. I'm hungrier this morning than normal.

After breakfast, I head to the stalls to ready Gunpowder. I take an extra moment to brush him slowly. I pay attention to his smooth black-gray hair and then saddle him.

Gunpowder lifts his head from the grain bucket, and his ears perk up in alert. Somebody is coming up the road. Turning around, I see Fin bound over the hill toward me. My smile grows as he runs circles around my legs, lowering his body, wagging his large gray tail, and raising his haunches in the air. He wants to play. I bat at his nose, and he jumps to the side. Playful snarls echo in his hollow muzzle. Chuckling to myself at his soft pawing, I let him get closer and then reach down and hug him around the neck.

He nuzzles into the crook of my neck and this makes me laugh out loud. The sound coming from me surprises and startles me. The lightness is shocking. I realize how stupid I must look and stand up quickly. Clearing my throat and straightening my jacket, I look at Aponi on her brown faithful horse, Almond.

"Morning," she says in greeting.

"Morning," I reply.

"You ready?"

I nod without a word.

I pull myself onto Gunpowder's muscled back and pat his white mane. With a soft click of my tongue, he starts up. He hasn't been as responsive to me lately but this morning he is minding me better than he has in months.

"How did last night go?" She does not turn her head as she takes the lead just slightly. I allow this because I'm not about to show her my panning spots.

"It was fine." She did not ask me any specifics so I do not elaborate. Again, I get the sense I want to hide that part of myself from her.

"You look better today. Did you eat something?"

"Yes, I got up and had a good breakfast," I say, wondering why she is checking in on me yet again.

"Did you go out with Logan last night?" She side-eyes me, waiting for a response.

I wince slightly. "I did, but only for a little bit. I came home before everyone else. They'd seen enough of me the night before."

Aponi nods.

Her silence makes my heart race a beat. Hungover and raw, I feel the need to explain myself more, "I felt bad about saying I would go and then bailing out at the last minute. Those guys don't let me live anything down, so I had to just show my face, you know?"

Observing Aponi, I look and wait for her disapproval. I figure she does not particularly approve of the Clancy Gang. I never see her out drinking for more than one drink here and there, so I assume she wouldn't approve of my nightly activities. I wait for the lecture.

"Did you have fun?" she asks.

Blinking at her, I consider this. "I mean, I guess I did. I still didn't feel the greatest. The amount of shit I got from them was rough, but I deserved it. So you know, it's all part of the fun."

"Before you went, did you want to go?" Aponi asks.

I hesitate before saying, "Oh, I don't know, but not showing my face would've been worse the longer I avoid it. It's better to take your licks than run and hide from them. They come anyway so might as well get them over with. Right?" I huff out a dry laugh and give her a half-smile. Self-deprecation usually helps to get people off my back.

She does not say anything as we continue in silence. I am relieved she drops it. I settle into the rhythm of the ride.

The sun hits my eyes as it crests the mountain ridge. The jagged line glows an amber-gold, making the mountain come alive and almost sing. I regret I have missed so many of these mornings.

Aponi guides us along the riverbed to an area I have panned thousands of times. Looking at her, I question her skills, knowing this is not a place where a gold vein will lead. She climbs down off of Almond and lets him graze in the grass nearby. I do the same with Gunpowder and wait for Aponi's lead.

I have not panned for weeks, so I suppose it is fine to start here just to get my bearings. God, it has been so long since these steps felt natural. When I let my list of chores get too long, I let my old, good habits go by the wayside. While it's been a nice break from it all, it also feels good to be back—back to myself. Back to moving my muscles in a way I trained them to move.

Aponi starts to pan and search. She has a different set of steps to get ready. She has more metal buckets than I have ever used. She sets them up in a row, three in total. Raising one eyebrow unconsciously, I walk away from her and start surveying the land the way I have done thousands of times but I already knew this bend so well my logic pokes at me. *This is a waste of time.*

Aponi appears to be in her own world. She doesn't seem to care that the current is too fast, or that this part of the river has been worked over by many panhandlers. She just focuses right in front of her as if she doesn't care what is going on around her or really what I'm doing. We continue on this way for more than an hour.

Finally, I get into the natural flow. My sloshing feels more fluid and focused. The cold water, silt, and pebbles feel rough and welcoming to my fingertips. Rushing water and chirping birds lighten my mood.

I see a moose cow and her twin baby calves drink from the river. Their long necks and legs meander in and out of the riverbed. Momma moose keeps an eye on us but apparently doesn't deem us a threat, so they continue to enjoy the river along with me. Fish brush their slimy bodies past my legs. Their rainbow colors refract against the morning sun and the clear crisp water, creating dimension and layers.

Absorbing more of this beauty, I forget what I am supposed to be *doing*. *More wasted time.* Not that I have been particularly productive lately, anyway, but being consciously aware of squandering my day grates at me worse in these moments.

Daddy and I worked this bend of the river early on in my childhood. Exhausting days on end with him already verified no vein is here. *So what am I doing here?* If I have no objective outcome, what is the Goddamned point? Reaching for the flask in my left chest pocket, I sneak a drink, making sure my back is turned to Aponi.

Aponi is sloshing through the water with her pan onto the shore yet again. I have not left the water once. I assess her a bit closer as she separates part of her findings into each one of the three buckets.

Not finding anything substantial enough to keep, I wonder if she's found a gold pocket. Sometimes the winter run-off can move pockets around, so I tromp out of the river to her.

"Did you find a pocket?" I ask.

"No, not really." She continues with her task of adding water to her pan. She has expert hands and techniques. She can add, swirl, and discard fast and it's impressive. She's even faster than Daddy.

I move closer to her. Scooping another shovel full, I see tiny gold flecks. I clean, swirl, and uncover three small pebble-sized gold nuggets. *Nope, not big enough.* I throw them all back to the river.

Shoving the blade of my shovel back into the earth, I jump in response to Aponi as she hollers at me.

"Girl, what are you doing?"

One of my brows raises while the other dips, and I lean slightly away. "What are you talking about now?"

"I saw what you threw back. Those were perfectly good," she says with an exasperated puff.

Confused, I look back at the river. Those were nothing—practically dust. Reaching into my pocket, I finger the gold nugget I've kept there from the day I pushed Daddy into the river and hold it out to show her. "This is what I am looking for. I throw back anything smaller than this."

She gets closer to me, takes in the size of my gold, and her eyes widen. She shakes her head at me and stomps over to her line of buckets. I follow her simply because I want to see what she has been doing all morning.

She points to the buckets. "Look, this is what I have found so far."

I peer in and see the bottom of each bucket is no longer visible. Whole layers of gold cover them—one with dust, one with pebbles, and then one with larger chunks. Nothing is as large as the nugget I hold limply at my side, yet all together, they look much more impressive. Each bucket glistens back at me from the morning sun, still wet from the river.

"You found all this just this morning?" Bending at the waist, I get a closer look. The piles are all made up of nuggets and dust about the size I just discarded without a second thought.

Aponi plops to the ground and wipes her brow. A single bead of sweat rolls down the side of her face. She has been moving much more than me, working up a sweat. I sit down next to her and continue to finger the gold nugget in front of me. Its dense weight feels lighter than it used to. This source of measurement shaped my perspective for years, yet now it seems lonely and insignificant. Aponi's eyes are on me again but I do not meet them.

"Ellie, you throw back everything smaller than that?" She points to the singular nugget in my hand. I nod once and then crane my neck back at her buckets, taking in all her steady progress.

She starts again when I don't say anything. "A lot of people around here are obsessed with 'striking gold' but I get to strike gold every day. For me, gold mining is a way of life. I use it to meet my needs, and Fin and I don't need much. If I had much more, I am not sure I would want to deal with it. I use what I find here to buy what I can't get on my own from these mountains and that's it."

"Yeah well, that is one way to look at it, I guess," I say. "But just think what a big gold strike would mean, Aponi? You could have it all. Freedom to do what you want. Respect from them all." My heartbeat quickens at the excitement of the possibility.

"Ellie, I have everything I want. I still enjoy hunting to feed myself and Fin. I do not need respect from anyone except myself. I already have the freedom to do what I want, when I want, and how I want." She pauses and considers. "And the reality of a gold strike would bring more people and trouble my way. So even if I struck it big, I would not want any part in it. That is not my definition of success." She then gets up and goes back to work.

Following her and staying close, I watch as she flicks her wrist quickly and with smaller motions. She demonstrates how to swirl so I don't lose the smaller particles—a technique I never had any interest in mastering. I can't believe how much gold I must've thrown away over the years.

    I consider her words for the rest of the morning. My past consisted of all-or-nothing thinking. Either you won or you lost. If it wasn't big enough, it wasn't good enough. Yet Aponi's words paint a gentler approach—one where success and contentment come to her daily. The word *content* has always seemed so inadequate to me. Yet this woman protected it. A little bit over time creates balance, ease, and freedom. Isn't that what we were all pushing for? To find enough safety and security to go from surviving to thriving?

    She seems to use this mindset as a way to maintain the life she chooses to live on her terms. The power she holds over her life is not something I have ever considered possible for a woman. I don't fit the ideal image of a woman in any way but neither does she. Yet she is demonstrating a different way of doing things.

    At this point in my life, I have never even considered what I want out of life. I was told how it would be, and that was the end of that. These past two days with Aponi make me question everything—from how I look at things down to the very way I want to spend my day. Even the way I want my coffee has me thinking about my desires and needs.

    I smile to myself as I decide, *Tomorrow, I'll have coffee with cream and no sugar.*

CHAPTER 24

Like the solid ground away from a cliff's edge, seeing Aponi and Fin each morning soothes me. We create a rhythm together that is new and easy. Fin and I ritualistically play and nuzzle when we see each other. Then I slip him a scrap of smoked or raw meat. Afterward, Aponi and I decide what we want to do each day. I don't think about my family or my loneliness as much when I am with them... until something reminds me of them.

We always make it back each morning before opening, which is much easier now that I've changed it to ten in the morning. Since making this decision, I do not loathe the task of taking care of the shop as much as I once did when the opening time was set at eight. My new hours are from ten in the morning to five at night, and because of this, I feel like I've gained part of my life back.

This chosen adjustment gives me time to drink an extra cup of coffee *with extra cream and no sugar*, read, journal, or just take time to enjoy the silence. Time by myself has become a priority for me. The space that used to feel like a black hole now feels cozy—not completely serene, but safer.

I initially felt automatic pangs of guilt when a customer knocked on the door before ten, but this only lasted for a few weeks. The rumor has quickly spread that my hours have been adjusted. During this transition, I braced myself for insults and side-eyes about my new hours but they never come. Even Logan resorts to a few snide remarks that quickly die out since I don't give them any energy.

Like ripples in a glassy pond, these miniature changes reverberate through my life. Releasing myself from the old patterns feels rebellious and peaceful all at once. These freeing feelings motivate me to look at every aspect of my life and question, *Is this really what I want?* It's still an effort to question the way things are, but with this perspective, I am able to look at my life from a whole new angle.

What was easier for me to identify at first was what I did not want. I didn't want to feel like I was just surviving. I didn't want to have so much pain anymore. I didn't want to be afraid anymore. Once I became clear on what I did *not* want, I was able to sift through to discover what I *did* want out of my life.

Once my desires become clearer, I can start painting a new life on the canvas of my choosing; it feels liberating to be the artist for once. Just like any new artist, though, I'm still learning to trust myself. My strokes are shaky at times.

Logan and I continue to meet up during the evenings, but the frequency has dwindled over time. I realize how much I value sleep and mornings more than the haze of a night out, the chaos, and the trouble that follows. Logan is coming over by himself now because I request, no, *demand it*. I no longer want to be around Tricia or the rest of them. However, I do still allow Logan to drive the loneliness away. I'm not ready to give up all my vices just yet.

Honestly, the full brunt of my reality would have consumed and crushed me if I brought it all into focus at once. For now, these little changes feel empowering and are all I can handle. I know I'll have to deal with bigger choices in the near future but for now, I'm content with putting this off. Frankly, they scare the *shit* out of me.

Aponi and I decide to head up the mountain to get a better vantage point. The caps of the mountains on the highest peaks are still dusted with snow and remain that way most of the year. Looking at the vast wilderness brings wonder and awe to my soul. I feel a deep sense of peace settle down my back as my muscles release and respond to my body dismounting Gunpowder.

We tie the horses to trees and continue by foot up the ridge. The soil under our leather boots is spongy from the morning dew. The fresh masculine scent of the evergreens, moss, and soil fills the air.

Aponi points to a clearing on the ridge and I nod, silently acknowledging this is a good hunting spot. Lately, we are hunting for what we need, so that means we target smaller game to feed ourselves and Fin. I no longer have to feed a whole family, and I recently accepted trade from other locals who don't mind processing the meat.

Releasing the responsibility for my sisters' survival was a struggle at first, but once I did, I realized how much I don't miss it. Admitting that they may actually be safer where they are, even if that is not with me, still sends pangs of guilt through my chest. I'm not sure guilt will ever *not* be part of me.

I still feel responsible for my sisters, though, so if I find a particularly handsome rabbit, fox, or grouse, I'll take the shot and send the pelt down to Maggie whenever Tommy comes up for a trade. Only sending the most beautiful and unique animals to my sisters calms the critical voice in my head.

When I send the hides down, Maggie sends finished coats, hats, boots, or gloves for me to sell. I overprice these items until I know another shipment is coming. This way, I have something of hers in the shop at all times. It's the last little bit of connection and communication we have.

Tommy didn't mention Graham yesterday when he came to trade, and I didn't ask. Apparently, Daniel is doing much better and Maggie and Lottie are fine. Missing my sisters hit me harder every time I receive an update. The double-edged blade of wanting to hear from her and then hearing and the slithering shame, anger, and loneliness that follows is still too much to bear.

I miss them so much.

As I position myself on the ground, I consider maybe I will make a trip to town someday soon, but then I immediately dismiss it; I'm not ready for that reunion.

Snapping from my whirling thoughts, I focus on hunting. We either shoot a deer or something larger together and share it or we each shoot something smaller like a turkey or grouse. It's been a while since we've scored a larger mark, and I've been craving something a little heartier. So when I see Aponi pass up two turkeys, a fox, and a rabbit, this indicates we're on the same hunt today for richer meat.

Just then, we hear a crashing mass descending the steep terrain. The power from the force pushing through the underbrush is effortless. The hair on the back of my arms stands up from the anticipation, and I slow my breathing.

Lumbering out into the clearing comes the silkiest and blackest bear I have ever seen. The fur catches the light and is so dark it appears blue, iridescent, and magnificent. I've never shot a bear, so this is my chance.

Lifting my gun, I don't think. I just react. Aiming, I shoot the beast right through the side—just behind the shoulder blade. The bear drops heavily to the forest floor. My worth and guilt sated with the size of my kill, I turn to my partner to celebrate, but her face does not light up. My gut hitches.

"Aponi, that is the biggest most handsome bear I have seen." Elated but wary, I wait for her response, hoping it will elevate with mine.

She simply answers, "I can agree with that."

Aponi rises up, dusts her pants off, and starts walking down the ridge to our horses. I follow. I know we will need them both to pack my bear out. We mount our horses and head down to where the bear lies waiting. Aponi remains silent the entire descent into the valley. We approach the bear and the size of the beast sinks in. I finally realize why Aponi is so quiet. How the hell are we going to get this giant back?

I panic and feel unsure about what to do next. No way will we be able to pack out this bear in one piece. Drawing out my knife, I start to skin the hide. She follows my lead and we work together at opposite ends. The intensity of the kill still lingers in my system, pairing with the tension between Aponi and me. I feel wired and on edge.

I've had enough. My nerves are fraying. "Hey, what is your problem?"

I continue to work through the fur and gore with a vengeance. Sweat rolls down my back as the heat of the day and my internal struggle builds rapidly.

"In my opinion, this kill was not needed. But we are here now and in this together," she replies matter-of-factly.

What am I supposed to say to that?

Wounded at the clear disappointment in her tone, I double down. This is not *her* responsibility. It is mine. *We* are not anything other than two lonely women on the mountain. She doesn't owe me anything.

"I don't need your help," I spit out. "Since this is such a *burden* to you, you can leave whenever you want. Isn't that what you are preaching to me all the time—freedom of choice?"

Aponi puts her knife down and pulls out her water skin. She drinks from it before replying, "I want to help. This is my choice. Even if it is not something I would have killed, that does not mean I would leave you here to deal with it alone."

Feeling guilty and self-righteous all at once, I throw back at her, "Well, what if I said that I don't want your help? That I am sick of your help and all your bullshit words. I am sick of you questioning everything I do."

Looking back down at the bear, I take my anger out on the flesh and focus on separating the fat from the muscle. The smell of the ripe kill fills my nostrils; I hate this part of hunting. Maggie always dressed the meat. Now that she's gone, I have to do it all. Resentment boils back up in my blood under my skin; the prickling presence returns.

Aponi pauses and waits as my eyes reluctantly meet hers.

"Ellie, I can be mad at you for taking this kill *and* I can understand why you did it."

"I killed that bear just like any sane hunter would," I spit back.

Aponi does not take the bait. "You are still learning. Sometimes your old thinking patterns will just take over. But you know better now. You know you can decide what you will do in the future. You'll make mistakes as you learn who you are, but you'll also choose more consciously. You might need to shoot a bear for many reasons, so why did you really pull the trigger?"

My jaw clenches and heat prickles under my skin, but her calm voice makes it difficult to lash out. She waits for my response.

"I don't know," I say uncomfortably and think about it for a while. "It's in me to pull the trigger. More was always better. Bigger was always better. Maggie had also passed through my mind. Is that so wrong?"

"The problem is not about considering others. It's in the motivation behind it. You miss your sister, and you haven't talked to her about it yet. So, am I correct in assuming you saw a way to connect with her by giving her something big, important, and impressive? But why? To prove you still love her? To validate your worth? To prove that you could take down a great beast?

"No gift will reconcile the rift in your relationship no matter how big it is. Pair that with the fact you now need to deal with the consequences of your kill. You need to process it—a task I know you do not like doing. We now have too much meat to consume ourselves, so either we eat ourselves sick with bear meat for weeks, we sell it, or we most likely waste it."

Bear meat is very rich and most people don't really even like it, I remember.

She continues, "You see, the same act can be good or bad. It all depends on the intention. What I want for you is the power to know yourself enough to make these choices with awareness. To not just react out of old patterns but to choose in alignment with the person you want to be. You have safety, money, skills, and shelter. Now you get to intentionally choose your actions. As your friend, that's all I want for you.

"Also, being both mad *and* supportive at the same time are both simultaneously true. Just because you upset me does not mean I don't want to be here for you. And guess what? You can be mad at me too, and that's fine."

I'm speechless. I'm still not used to this kind of talk, and it makes me feel uncomfortable. But it also makes me feel safe at the same time. I still want to bolt, push her away, or lash out so she *will* leave me. All of these techniques used to work for me in the past. Using my shields to protect myself feels more familiar. But if I'm being really honest with myself, it's also the reason I'm so alone and miserable.

Until about three weeks ago, I felt numb and dead inside. But over time, I have started to live and now participate in my life instead of letting life bounce off of me. I'm no longer aimlessly existing. I still don't like these conversations, especially now that she considers me her friend. But I also know if I want something authentically my own—if this was a true core desire—I would have to do things differently.

Sitting on the forest floor, I point my shoulders at Aponi, and with all my heart, I say, "I am sorry for putting you into this situation. I was not thinking. I just miss Maggie and Lottie. I miss Graham, and I don't know how to fix it. I'm not ready to deal with all of this. I'm so angry at everyone. I'm angry at Momma for dying. I'm angry at Daddy for deserting us—for betraying me. I'm angry at him for choosing alcohol and pride over his family and I'm angry at all the rest of them for leaving me. But most of all, I'm so angry at myself I can hardly stand it."

Aponi takes me in as her whole body softens. "I see more sadness than anger in those beautiful eyes."

She really sees me. Then I completely lose it. Tears stream down my face as the sadness and pain flood over me.

The death grip on my anger is something I can deal with. I know anger, physical fighting, yelling matches, and cussing. But I'm not accustomed to sadness. Sadness is weak and not okay; it is indulgent. No one ever sees me cry. Anger is acceptable, not sadness.

Falling back from my knees to my butt, I drop my knife to the ground. Covering my face with my hands, I can't hold it in anymore. Blood smears my face, but I don't care. The river I keep tightly dammed up inside me breaks free. The grief rushes through my core, icy and sharp.

The stream of tears falls for what seems like an eternity. Aponi comes over to me, wraps her arms around my shoulders, and holds me. She holds my body and gives me the space I need to get this thing out of me. I had never allowed another person to see me like this and there's no going back.

"It is not your fault, Ellie. It was never your fault." She caresses my hair.

My sobs rack my body, and I let them consume me. I am sweaty, wet, and covered in blood. I didn't believe I could ever sink to these depths. But as I allow myself to break, the heavy weight finally lifts off my shoulders. Aponi witnesses me in my most shattered state, and she doesn't sneer, push me away, or look uncomfortable. She accepts me as I am—at this moment. All the blood, sweat, and tears don't faze this strong woman I now call my friend. She holds me and trudges through it all with me.

"As painful as this is, Ellie, this is the way through to a much lighter and fulfilling life. Notice how you feel now in this moment. Was it worth it?" she asks earnestly.

I peer at her through my wet dark lashes as I take a deep inhale. "I can breathe, Aponi. I didn't realize I wasn't breathing until now."

My tear-lined eyes finally stop streaming. The world around me looks different. I just went to the place I was most terrified to face and came out clearer. This feeling and the release of pressure burst out of me like the steam from a train stopping at the station. Just like the vapors, I feel powerful, hot, and strong.

I wipe my face with the sleeve of my brown leather jacket, the one that Maggie made especially for me, and I smile at it with love. Resentment eases away and only compassion swells. It can be different for me, and there's no going back. I now know a better way, and I'm willing to do the difficult things I must do to get there.

Aponi and I return to the bear. We work together, dressing and sectioning off the flesh. As I work, my wants and needs become clearer. Things can be different, and for the first time, I am excited about the unknown possibilities of the future.

CHAPTER 25

How many ways can one person punish themselves? Logan's company has been a salve to the tumor of my loneliness. He distracts me from my miserable reality, but that no longer serves me. I now see how he salted my wounds and how I let him. I even refilled the shaker myself on multiple occasions.

Contemplating this break has been on my mind all day and most of the week. Once I make this break, I will truly be alone. Aponi and Fin are here, but they can't fill the hole in my heart.

After all the time I've spent with Aponi and taking back my life, this decision to cut Logan off is inevitable. I need to speak to the ones I deeply hurt, but before I do this, I need to make space for the possibility of a life with them.

Logan will stop by tonight since we haven't seen each other for several days. I've intentionally spent more nights at Aponi's for dinner to avoid this conflict, but now it's time to face reality. I make myself busy in the shop by cleaning up from the day. I'm now only open four days a week with reduced hours, but I still begrudgingly do the chores. I'm just not meant to be a shop owner.

Outside, hoofs approach the cabin. My heart pounds in my chest. From the kitchen window, I see Logan tying his reins to the post near the door before entering without a knock.

"Hey, El. You still open?"

Obviously, I am. I haven't flipped the *open* sign yet, and the door is not locked. So I don't even reply. He saunters over to where I restock the pickled goods.

"I'm surprised. Your shop is hardly ever open anymore. You know people are startin' to talk." He leans his back against the shelves directly in my way.

I try to not let that dig get under my skin. He doesn't understand my newer decisions. He doesn't have to. I don't need him or anyone else to understand my choices anymore.

"I'm thinking about closing altogether. I never liked this part of the business, anyhow. And now that Maggie is gone, I'm not sure I want to keep it going," I say as I continue to stock shelves around his body.

"Where are we gonna get our supplies from, honey?" he asks incredulously.

I shrug. "In town—like we all used to. Or maybe I'll sell it to someone who would be interested in keeping the shop. This place is too big for one person, anyway."

He slides closer to me, connecting our hips, our faces inches away. "I could help you fill it up."

Placing my hand on his chest, I push away to make space for myself. If we get too close, I will fall prey to the same ending we have tumbled into for the last several months. His hard muscled chest and sharp tongue seduce me even now. I know why I used him and he used me. We have a perfectly dysfunctional relationship that can replicate what I knew and grew accustomed to. It's truly enticing to fall back into the pillow of the past.

"Logan, I can't anymore." I move away from him, which gives me more confidence to speak my mind. My chest tightens. I sense this isn't going to go well.

"What do you mean? The shop? Sure you can. No one actually cares that you changed the hours. As long as you keep it open, people will deal," he says without much thought.

"I'm not just talking about the shop. I'm talking about you and me. I can't do this anymore. I don't want to."

He reaches for me and grabs both of my wrists. His thumbs press into the tender inner flesh as he pushes me up against the wall and whispers into my ear, "Oh, come on, Ellie. I know you want it. You like this thing we have. You need me."

He pulls one of my bound wrists to his mouth and bites it playfully before kissing where he left the teeth marks. My core tightens. My desire is there, but my heart isn't. I'm fearing that a part of me would miss this, and I hesitate. I need more space. Pulling my arm away, I side-step behind the counter.

"Our time together *was* what I wanted and needed, but now I want more than what you can give. And I can't give you what you want. This world you live in is not what I want. I tried it, and I do not like the person I became when I was with you. I am who I am, and you are who you are. We can't be together, and that is what I want. This thing between us is over."

Leaning over the counter, he shoots back, "This is that Indian woman's fault. She has changed you. You act like you're better than the rest of us now. We know you, Ellie. You are one of us."

"I have changed but this is me. I have been hiding behind all of this." I motion to him and the shop. "It's not who I want to be. I'm a mountain woman and always will be but not in the way that brings you here each night. I can't be that for you." I make direct eye contact then with more confidence.

"So, you're actually going to leave this mountain and go after him? Is that it? You really think he is going to be interested in a roughneck, used-up slut like you?" he says as he runs a finger up my arm.

Snatching my arm away, I cross it over my body to protect myself. Disgust for this man rips through me. *I am not a slut. I am not a slut. I am not a slut,* I silently tell myself.

"Logan, I have given myself to you. And I'm not sure if he or any other man will be interested in me after that. But I don't regret it and you can't make me feel bad about this anymore," I say, jutting my chin out for emphasis.

"Oh, I won't be the one that makes you feel bad about this, Ellie. Not only Graham but the townies have heard all about it. Everyone knows who you are. Even if Graham does take you back, you'll never be accepted by them. They'll shun you. Graham will have to pretend not to hear the whispers about how his wild woman spread herself around."

His vicious smile does not reach his eyes. He's using his most poisonous venom now.

"That might be true. Even if that does happen, I would rather be alone and truthful to myself and those I love than hide out here with you and waste my life away. You are bad for me, and I know that now. I don't need you. I don't *want* you. Now *get out.*" Squaring my shoulders, I point my finger at the door.

His eyes narrow. "Ellie, if you leave here, I cannot promise I won't be forced to find another pastime closer to town. It's been so peaceful with this shop, but if you are not here to keep us stocked, I'm not sure what will happen. You remember what it was like before? Those times may return if you aren't careful." His threat hangs between us.

He knows exactly what to say to keep me small. I've used these same excuses to keep myself here, too, but I know now this isn't the only way things can be.

"Logan, that is a choice you and the others will have to make for yourselves. If that is the way you want to live, I can't stop you. It's not my job, and it never was."

He meanders around the counter toward me. I can feel the heat from his body and his breath on my face as he leans in next to my ear, his lips caressing the curve. "That sister of yours is still single and would make a fine pastime. It'll be like being with you but softer... better. She isn't tainted *yet*. I could help her become a woman, too."

Revulsion coils in my stomach, and I push him in the chest with both of my hands. "Don't you touch my sister, you fucking bastard!"

Logan laughs. "There's my Ellie. You'll never change, and when you figure that out, come and find me."

Logan will never admit it, but I can see the hurt in his eyes. Regaining my composure, I walk to the door and open it for him. Logan makes his way toward me.

Lowering his voice, he growls, "Remember, you did this."

Mounting his horse, he kicks hard and gallops off. My heart is still racing. The conversation starts to replay in my mind but I stop it. His words strike a chord, but I know deep down he's wrong. I now believe I can have a different life. I've learned over the last several months that my mind will reiterate all those hurtful words, but I will no longer accept or tolerate this kind of treatment from myself or anyone else.

I stand alone in that cabin with a sense of pride and confidence that only I can give myself. I no longer allow people to speak to me like this, and that's final.

CHAPTER 26

Three weeks have passed since I cut Logan out of my life. A sense of peace trickles through my body because of it. I no longer wait for him with hope or fear. My life is now occupied with soul- and energy-filling activities from my own personal menu. I spend most of my time reading, being with Aponi, or taking long baths. I take walks for enjoyment and only hunt when I want to. I even catch myself humming and singing at times. Although I am finding moments of contentment, a heavy sorrow still weighs me down.

I don't want to admit it, but I miss them all, especially Daddy. I miss our time together and our relationship—even if it was not always the best. Knowing he created his own cage to protect himself made me less angry but sorrowful for his limited understanding of his worthiness. I had done the same so my compassion could encompass us both. I am no longer mad at him, my momma, my sisters, Graham, or even myself.

Yet the sadness still sits low in my gut. The pit in my stomach appears to be the last chain link shackling me in place. Reality continues to sink in. I can no longer rely upon any of them to return. I have to face it. They're gone.

Honestly, it all still hurts so much. I no longer have Logan, alcohol, or the distraction of caring for my sisters blurring or blunting the truth. So at times, old toxic ways still seem alluring. The ease of shutting all these big feelings off used to be right at my fingertips. I no longer keep alcohol at the cabin, but my hands still itch to open the door where I once kept my liquid escape. Old ways still seem to flick on just like a match being lit.

This evening, I plan to eat dinner at Aponi's, but it's only just after lunch and much too early. Trying to calm my nerves, I repeat to myself, *I am enough as I am. I am enough as I am. I am enough as I am.*

I still need to remind myself of this truth and wonder tiredly if it will ever become something I actually believe. For now, convincing myself is a daily—sometimes hourly—reminder.

My loneliness and despair consume me. My skin is crawling, my gut roiling and wriggling as if it's begging me to unravel. I have been here before but at this moment, it feels as if I am struggling to keep my head above water. I don't get pulled under the current anymore, but I still think I'm learning how to keep my head above water and paddle at the same time.

I mount Gunpowder and unconsciously point us in the direction of the tavern. Yet once we hit the fork in the road, he turns us toward Aponi's instead. I let him lead us to our safety.

Gunpowder knows the way and carries us quickly. He knows he'll get an apple when we arrive. I place him in the stall next to Almond, who steps aside to share her hay. I reach for the ripe red apples and hand one to each horse. They munch on their apples and then start to groom each other. My lips twitch up at yet another example of how much life has changed for us.

Aponi is out tending her flowers. She's the only one with an immaculate garden but also has flowers just for her own pleasure. Her roses are her pride and joy, and her wrinkled skilled hands are busy pruning the dead heads.

On her knees and in the dirt, her neck lifts up. Her smile goes to her eyes when she is really happy. I love that they do that as our eyes meet.

"You're here early."

"That cabin was closin' in on me. I needed to get out of there," I say, no longer trying to pretend to be anything but what I am—especially with her. I kick the dirt and shift my weight from one foot to the other.

"What's eatin' at you, girl?" she asks, turning back to her task.

Guilt about bothering her during her task gnaws at me still but I brush it off. I still struggle with needing so much support.

"I can't shake this sadness. I feel like it was easier being mad all the time. Now I'm just sad. Why am I sad about something that never was?"

She simply nods her head once and continues to listen.

"Daddy is never coming back. I know I can't have Momma or my sisters like I used to have them. I feel like I'm losing a part of myself. I know it doesn't make sense since I'm still here. The thought of leaving this place still seems unimaginable, though. I don't know if I will ever be able to leave. I have to admit Logan's threat plays into these feelings. The safer option is to stay here. Why can't life just be easier?"

Aponi chops another dead limb off as she continues to work. She lets the silence hang between us for a few moments. "Here, Ellie, I want you to help me with this." She hands me a pair of sheers to make my job easier.

"Look here. You see where the damaged part is?" She lifts a crooked blackened thorny branch with a crumbling dark red bud. "You see where the healthier thicker branch is? This is the bit of the plant we want to salvage." Under all the black and darkness, I see a vibrant, soft, youthful, green vine with the edges of a healthy red bud peeking out.

"You have to cut out the old branches to make way for the newer ones." Our eyes meet.

Understanding the double meaning, I chop off the plant where she points with one clean slice. I continue to easily identify the other parts of the plant that need excising.

She continues, "There cannot be rebirth without death. The seasons remind us of this as does the loss of the way you thought life would be. But without this process, there would not be space for the new."

"I get making room. It's why I got rid of Logan, but the death part I don't understand. I haven't died. I only lost the mere idea of how I thought my life would be."

"Parts of you did die, Ellie. Right now, you are experiencing the death of the way things were. This is why many people never even get to where you are now. The thought of killing off life as they know it would be too much. It's why they stay stuck as they are. They don't even get to the point of dreaming of what could be. You are not alone, I have experienced this too. Many times my expectations were different than what life had planned for me. All my life, I wanted to be a mother, but it just never happened for me. I had to grieve this loss and the idea of being a mother, letting go of the life that could've been and how it would not and could not be mine. This release did not happen overnight, but it did happen with time. Time takes time, Ellie."

While we work, Aponi continues, "The idea of something is just as real as the actual having of it, and our hearts do not know the difference. We have to allow our hearts and soul to feel these losses so our minds can process them and move through them to accept what actually is. But you can't bypass this grief—even if the possibility of the future seems hopeful."

"But what if the unknown isn't better?" I want reassurance.

"Then it is not your end. It's just part of your story," she says confidently and without hesitation.

I lift my black hat and rake a hand through my hair. "Shit, Aponi, is hope enough to hang on to? To give all this up, all that I know, for something that might be?" I desperately ask as my heart starts to pound and the tears burn in my eyes, threatening to burst over.

"You tell me, Ellie. Is it?"

I consider this as a single hot heavy tear slides down my face. All the hurt and the work I had done to get to this place has been grueling. I still wish things could have been different. I wish I could have protected my family from all harm and hurt, but I don't have that kind of power or control. Surrendering to life as it is, rather than life as I imagined it to be, is almost impossible to consider. But my hands have become so bloody and raw from gripping the fraying rope of life, trying to control the speed at which it fell, I have no choice but to let it go.

I once wanted to make everyone proud, but I now want to make myself proud more. I want to love and have a life that is my own. I want authenticity, connection, and adventure.

That knot in my belly begins to untangle as I unload it all. I would never have the past image of my life, but the unknown hope of what might be has me answering my friend confidently, "Yes, it is worth it."

Aponi's smile spreads across her face and into her eyes again. "Ellie, if I had a daughter, I would've wanted her to be just like you." Her eyes well up, glistening.

Grabbing her hands in mine, meeting her kind and wise eyes with mine, I say, "You have a daughter." I pull her into me and let my body fully relax into hers.

We continue to prune her precious plants until dinnertime. After we feast, we burn the brush and celebrate the warmth it produces. As the flames reflect off our faces, the old Ellie dies and burns along with it. I allow the last strings of sorrow to fray completely for tonight because tomorrow it will be time for a new beginning.

COME WHAT MAY

CHAPTER 27

Last night, I prepared for the journey to town as if I was packing for a hunt. My fingers easily remembered to secure my gun, store my food, and tie on extra layers—all routine tasks I have repeated thousands of times. This morning, though, once all the methodical duties are completed, all I've got to do is close our shop.

It's more difficult than I imagined. This is still my home and all the memories it holds are still a part of me. Tears spring to my eyes expectedly and sting the edges. They don't have time to spill over before a light knock on the door draws my attention away. I turn the bolt over and open the door to Aponi and a full-body wagging Fin. The tension in my neck dissolves, and I let her see the tears in my eyes without turning away.

"I thought you might want some help," Aponi said.

Reaching for her, I hold her to me with all my might.

"Thank you, for everything." I sniff into her neck.

She just grabs my face between her hands and smiles.

Together, we board up the windows and secure the exits. She finishes loading up all the perishables onto Almond with Fin at her feet.

Alone, I take in the big room one last time. Standing right in the middle, I appreciate the quiet space. The shelves are empty and shadowed. The kitchen table is without Maggie's decorative doily in the center. The chairs are all snuggly pushed under and tucked away. I take in one last breath through my nose and sigh out through my mouth before I leave and bolt the door behind me.

Words don't pass between Aponi and me until it is time for us to say our goodbyes.

Turning to her, my throat tightens and my breath hitches as I try to start. "Aponi... I, you..."

"I know. I know." Warmth permeates her. She grabs my hands. "I need to say one last thing."

Wiping my tears for what feels like the millionth time, I'm ready for her parting wisdom.

"There comes a time when you have to decide if your sad story defines you or drives you. You are not perfect. None of us are. We all have our own version of a sad story. Grief and recovery are not linear, but you will never be where you once were unless you choose to go back there. You can't unlearn what you now know is truly possible. So the direction is forward with back steps but never again at the bottom. Just like a backstitch in a quilt, those moments only strengthen your journey. You can be mad, sad, hurt, *and* be powerful, driven, and strong."

Aponi pulls our foreheads together. "Now go live your life, you beautiful, wonderful, powerful, strong, stubborn, loving, healing, whole woman."

We embrace for a long time. I want to remember this moment forever. Not only her words but the pride I feel for myself and how far I have come.

I pet and cuddle Fin as he leans in, wrapping his neck and tail around me one last time. I mount Gunpowder and direct us toward town and our future.

* * *

My stomach doesn't flip until I round the last corner of the trail that opens up into town. Imagining all the possibilities distracts me from my travels. Adventures with Graham, hugging my sisters, and the freedom to live my life send chills down my spine over and over again.

My reverie brings a proud swell in my chest as I realize I'm focusing on what might be me instead of running through all the conversations I am about to have. Normally by now, I would've practiced the conversation on repeat, attempting to predict every outcome possible. But not this time, not anymore.

Gunpowder and I saunter onto the main street. People walk together and make way for us but do not sneer or flinch at our presence. Others continue to window shop the bakery or toy stores and pay no attention to us. One couple even tips their chins at us. This is not the town I remember growing up in.

Maybe the change is in me, or in them, or just time. I am not sure but whatever it is, I don't feel so defensive.

This is progress. However, the old responses of tightening up, closing off, and protecting myself by becoming unapproachable still bubble up. I breathe in through my nose and out through my mouth to settle myself. I want calmness and presence so I am able to say what I mean instead of letting my nerves take the reins. I'm the conductor now—not the inner voice that even now tries to remind me *how stupid I am* for being here.

I silence my self-doubt by reminding it that I've got this. I have proven time and time again over the last several months that I can do this. The fact that I'm riding down the main street is enough to give me the confidence I need to move forward.

Tying Gunpowder to the mercantile's wood railing, I fill my chest with air and allow it deep into my belly one last time before my brown boots carry me through the mercantile threshold.

Overhead, the bell rings as I step into the mercantile and see Maggie making a sale.

"I will be right with you." Maggie continues to ring up the patron without looking up. Her face is relaxed and at ease.

I don't respond, not wanting to interrupt her. I watch her, my chest filling with pride as she finishes the transaction with a woman in a very fancy dress.

"Now, Maggie, you need to tell me when your next piece will be ready. I insist on first dibs." The fancy patron leans over the counter and touches my sister's arm.

Maggie smiles sweetly. "You know how I do it, Mrs. Walton. My new pieces go up for sale the first Thursday of every month."

The woman has glittering baubles hanging from her drooping earlobes, her neck layered with mixed metals, beads, and lockets. The wealthy Mrs. Walton looks hurt but her eyes sparkle with mirth. "If you gave me a preview now, I *know* I would make it worth your while. You can bend the rules just this once."

Maggie rounds the counter to hand the woman her parcel then grabs her by the elbow and gently guides the woman toward the door. "Well, that wouldn't be fair to the rest of the ladies. Now would it?"

"Oh, hush. You know I will pay the most, which *is* the fairest way to do things," Mrs. Walton pushes ruthlessly.

Maggie finally looks up at me, her eyes widening at first before light ripples across her face and sparkles there. Her expression softens at me standing before her.

Letting go of Mrs. Walton's elbow, Maggie rushes to me. Mrs. Walton's face quirks up, and her arched manicured black eyebrow follows. Likely she's trying to make sense of why Maggie, dressed in a light blue delicate, clean, and pressed dress, would have anything to do with the dirty and dusty mountain woman in leathers as she exits the mercantile.

The embrace is the crushing sort. We try to get closer and closer to make as much contact as we possibly can.

Maggie's soft sobs reverberate through her tiny frame.

"Oh, Maggie." Tears sting at my eyes. "If you start, I will too."

"I don't care," Maggie sobs into my hair.

The tension in my body melts away the second I have her in my arms. Little feet scamper toward me from across the room. Lottie thuds rapidly to us, and we both only break our connection long enough to let her in, lifting her between us both. Her little body adheres to mine and the scent of her thaws the last bits of my frozen fear.

As I lean back, my eyes meet Maggie's. "I am so sorry for pushing you away."

Maggie shakes her head. "No, I am sorry for turning my back on you."

"Maggie, it was the best choice either of us made in a long time."

"I just didn't know what else to do." Her sobs slow to soft hitches.

"I know," I say while wiping tears away.

Maggie shakes her head again. "I should not have left you."

Taking her firmly by the shoulder and still holding Lottie, I steady my voice. "I needed to find myself, or what was left of me, once I didn't have you. You two were all I had. I felt worthless without hiding behind taking care of you. I shouldn't have used you like that."

"You are a lot more than that," Maggie says with so much confidence it makes me smile.

"I know that now." My whole body feels steady and grounded as the words leave my mouth. This is another victory for me, to accept a compliment and believe it.

We finally pull away from the hug, but we remain close. I focus on my surroundings then and notice the front corner is filled with the most luxurious furs and clothing I have ever seen. Above it hangs the sign, *Maggie's Corner.*

"Maggie, are these all yours?" My eyes can't consume the exquisite material and sizes all at once.

My older sister beams. "Daniel cleared out this corner for me. I had all this room and space to fill. It was like once I had it to fill, the inspiration just poured out of me. We are staying in his guest room, and Daniel allows me to use his wife's old sewing room and machine. Her machine is an industrial grade, so my output is so much quicker. Materials are abundant here, and people pay top dollar for it all."

Maggie carries on, showing off all her new techniques, patterns, and displays. She has something for everyone. She even has a rack of rougher and tougher options for rugged women. I want every single article from that area. Maggie moves around the mercantile with a steady stride and her chin proudly set. It's obvious she feels at home.

"Maggie, you have a gift. You really do." Lottie finally allows me to put her down. Her little hand finds mine, and we walk around admiring Maggie's work.

"I feel like it's been bottled up inside for so long that it's just spilling out. Daniel keeps expanding my corner." Her cheeks stain pink at this.

"Uh-huh. What else is he making room for?" I tease her with my eyes.

"He is old-fashioned, Ellie, and for God's sake, he is healing," she says and then fans herself.

"Lips and hands can do a lot if you let them," I say, trying to get more information out of her.

"You." She bats at the air in front of her. Her other hand goes to her chest, and she smiles a big cat-like smile.

"But Daniel is healing. Right? Is he going to be okay?" I ask with genuine concern. I love to see Maggie so happy and don't want it taken away from her.

Lines furrow her brows. "He is doing much better but the doctor says he may never walk again without a cane."

This information directs my worries back to Graham. If Daniel can no longer walk, travel will be out of the question for months—if ever.

"Any word from Graham?"

"Tommy said Graham should be on his way back from the west route in just over a week," Maggie replies reassuringly.

I decide then and there that I can't wait that long. I need to see him sooner. My mind starts racing and distraction steals me from our conversation.

"Go to him." Maggie's voice breaks my loop.

Our eyes lock. I don't want to leave them so soon.

"We will be here, Ellie—when you *both* return." Her voice urges me to follow what I truly want to do.

"I am so scared to confront him. After all that's happened since we last spoke. I went somewhere dark, Mags. What if it was too much for him? What if I went too far?"

"Then he is a stupid man who doesn't deserve you," she says bluntly.

I choke on the laugh that bursts from me. I'm not used to my sister being so blunt.

"Maggie, this new life suits you."

"I know it does." Her grin stretches across her face.

My reunion with my sisters goes better than I could have ever hoped for. They are home, and I am finding mine. Warm calmness settles over my whole body now that I know both my sisters are cared for, safe, and thriving.

Now it's my turn to see if I have a chance at not just surviving but thriving as well.

CHAPTER 28

The majority of the weight on my chest lightens but doesn't completely dissipate after I say goodbye and hug my sisters one last time. Trying to calm myself, again, I look inward. My mind immediately wants to spiral into the depths of despair and replay all the fears I have of Graham shutting me down or saying he wants nothing to do with me.

Tommy points me west in the direction he is sure Graham is traveling from. Hoping Graham will only be a few days' rides away, I take off. The unknowing of if or when I will meet Graham is enough to set my nerves on edge.

The self-critical loops keep cropping up. *He won't want you. You are a harlot. No man will ever want you after what you've done. He deserves a pretty little wife who isn't so difficult.*

"Stop," I say out loud to myself. Catching this spiral of thoughts is part of the process. I don't let the negative whirlwind flip through my head freely like it used to. One day at a time sometimes feels too daunting, so one moment at a time is the survival rope I cling on to when I need it. At this point, I have a system to shut down these damaging thoughts.

Deep breaths first, in through my nose for a count of one, two, three, four, and then hold. Then out through my mouth for a count of one, two, three, four, five, six. Then hold and repeat. This slows my world down so I'm able to become present.

Next, I focus on what I can see. The vast beautiful landscape on the horizon. The purple hues on the snowy mountain peaks. Gunpowder's coarse gray mane. What can I hear? The gravel beneath Gunpowder's feet, his breathing, the birds chirping. What can I feel? The rich soft bridle leathers in my hands, the heavy coat and new clothes Maggie has given me. A large-brimmed light brown hat covers my head.

Slowly, this brings me back to myself. At this moment, I'm on a new trail, off the mountain, and moving toward a future. And no matter what happens, I'm doing it. I'm finally living.

No trouble confronts me on the road, but my senses are still primed for whatever may come my way. It is exhilarating. Noticing how much I love to ride, camp, hunt, and travel surprises me. These activities help me focus on the here and now instead of the conversation I might have soon with the love of my life.

I realize I really like the road. No, I love it. It's the perfect combination of all the things I value. Minimal supplies, hunting for food, being in nature, and sleeping under the inky black sky with infinite stars, and I have to admit the danger of the road make it that much more exhilarating to me. If Graham doesn't accept me, maybe I can find a place on the road doing something else. My possibilities are endless.

A wide smile spreads across my face. The amount of smiling and tears that make up a normal part of my life now still catch me off guard. It all still feels so new, but I'm enjoying the changing sensations—inner happiness and tears of joy instead of sorrow.

Gunpowder's ears perk up so I pull the reins. We stop to listen. Someone is coming toward us. Quickly, I dart us into the woods and hide Gunpowder. Running back, I position myself behind a fallen tree and wait for whoever is coming our way.

The large, covered wagon with four muscled horses travels up the road toward us, and my heart pounds out of my chest in response. It's him.

Graham's hat is atop his head and his rifle sits next to his side, ready for a fight at any moment.

My chest caves as I take in the look on his face—ragged, worried, and worn. His time away appears to have been hard on him, too. Quickly, I scan his broad shoulders and body; he looks unscathed and physically well.

The soles of my boots take off from under me before I can think. I step out onto the road and rip off my hat, allowing my dark hair to fall, the same way I did when he saved me that winter.

Graham pulls on the reins and his horses stop. His body straightens up and our eyes lock—just like they had so many years ago. Our eyes always have a way of finding each other. His deep stormy blues disarm me.

As I tentatively walk toward him, my hands start to tremble. I want to fill them with his hair and crush my lips against his sad and slightly open mouth, but I must use my words first.

Graham climbs down so we are finally face to face. He moves his sad, full lips like he is going to talk, but I hold up my hand.

Graham's eyes are serious and stoic. They don't let me in on what he is thinking or feeling. I harness my fears and use my bravery to maintain my strength to continue.

"I will never be the pretty wife who stays at home, and this can never be an expectation from you. I want to live and have adventures. I want to love passionately and be a partner. I'm never going to be a good cook and I have not decided on babies, but if it's something you want, I would consider it. I want to make love *and* have rough amazing sex. I want to sleep under the stars but also have a place to call home. I want to kill just for food and nothing else. I want to wear pants most of the time but sometimes I want to wear dresses too."

He waits patiently as I continue.

"Graham, I'm here in front of you asking for you to take me back as I am—my history and all. I realize now you are all there is for me. You are my equal. I just needed time to figure this out. I'm sorry I hurt you but I don't regret the choices I made. I needed to go there to see what I really wanted. Going there meant I did things I'm not proud of, but I needed to experience that to understand what we had. What I offer you includes my past, present, and future self. I'm proud of how far I've come. And I want you to understand that it had nothing to do with how you treated me but everything to do with how I treated myself. I understand if it's not what you want, but I refuse to be anything but myself."

Taking one last deep calming breath and standing in front of the man I love, I say, "And most of all, I want you to be mine now and forever."

Graham's voice is rough and raw, deep and gravelly like he hasn't spoken in a while.

"Finally," he sighs out. Hanging on to this single word, he pauses a long while and then climbs down from his wagon. "You finally see what I have seen all these years. You are all I want. You were always exactly what I wanted."

We both soften our stances and step another foot closer; the tension deliciously builds between us.

Graham continues, "I want you to know how much I've thought about you since the moment I left." He is now within arm's reach of me, and he reaches up and tucks a loose strand of hair behind my ear. His touch along the curve of my ear sends chills down my spine.

"Your face, your light, your fire—all of it traveled with me. I thought of how much you would love the road and how I wanted to share it with you. How we could keep each other safe, warm, and happy."

He continues to edge closer. "It has only ever been you and it will only ever be you. I want you, Ellie, right now and forever."

His strong hands grab my head right before his wanting lips crash down upon mine. My hands find his hair, and I lace my fingers through it and grab a handful. His smell and taste calm my senses completely. He feels like home.

Our bodies melt together yet I still feel there is too much space between us. His hands leave my neck and pick me up as I wrap my legs around him. He carries me into the forest, and we rip our clothes off, leaving a trail in our wake. The crisp fall air hits my bare skin, but I'm not cold as the sensations light me up.

Graham's hot tongue contrasts with the air and sends waves deep to my core. I need him now. Throwing his coat to the forest floor, he lays us down. We are not able to pull off the remaining clothes fast enough. Finally, he's over me and pauses.

He looks into my eyes and says, "I want to savor this moment. I want to watch you come undone with me. I want you."

"I want that too," I say, panting, ready, and wanting.

He slides himself into me slowly, and our eyes continue to lock and wordlessly communicate the desire burning between us. A sigh escapes my mouth as his eyes roll back.

He lifts my arching back and moves his hips just so he hits all the places I love. Graham allows me to build so I'm ready to explode. Softness before the thunder.

Our bodies press together, and he whispers in my ear, "You said you liked it rough?"

Graham doesn't wait for my response as he slams into me. I scream out as I come undone around him, feeling him finish with me. I release in a way I had been holding back from, coming to completion in the only way trust and surrender can achieve.

Both of us tremble as he rolls to his side but keeps an arm around me. As we catch our breath, Graham murmurs, "Is that what you were talking about?"

"Better than I could have imagined." I launch myself at him again.

CHAPTER 29

Three blissful days have passed since Graham and I made up. The continual makeup is mind-blowing. I hope we make up forever. Emotions scatter through our connection ranging from desperate removal of clothing, pushing, and releasing to caresses, holding, and talking about our future.

Happiness this intense still feels scary to me, and my self-consciousness threatens to close me back off. Graham can always seem to read my body tensing and relaxing, and he has a way of bringing me back to this bubble of paradise I can't believe is ours.

As we lay on the fur bedding, my breathing returns to normal once more after another finish. Rolling over to face him, I say, "I'm not sure I'm ready to be back in civilization."

He leans up on his forearm and kisses my temple before tracing a single finger down the curves of my body with a smile painted on his face. "We could stay out here for one more night."

My mood lifts. "Ummm, I think yes."

I want to stay out here with him forever. Closing my eyes, I allow his touch to relax me once more.

It's inevitable, though. Sooner or later, I need to tell Graham about our time apart. What I did, who I was with, who I'd become.

"Where are you, Ellie?" His deep voice brings me back.

My stomach flips and I force myself to take deep breaths. It is time.

"I want to talk about our time apart. I want to tell you before you hear it from anyone else."

"Ellie, I don't care what anyone says. You are a survivor. I know you did what you had to do to survive."

"That's the thing. I did things that were not about survival." I sit up and realize how on display I am. "Let's get dressed and then I'll tell you about it."

Graham's face scans mine warily. He hands me my shirt, and I hand him his pants. Our clothes were always as twisted up as us.

It's early morning as we leave the tent and continue to dress. I start a fire so I can boil water for coffee. Crouching down, I listen to the fire build and crackle. I'm trying to muster my courage with the flames as they began to climb. My greatest fear and thoughts of losing Graham try to flick at my confidence, but I shut them down before I can spiral backward.

Graham exits the tent and comes to stand right next to me, wrapping an arm around my shoulder, resting his head on mine, and nuzzling me in closer.

Exhaling through my nose, I start, "I was at the lowest moment of my life. Everything I loved was gone, and I felt like I had pushed it all away. I felt like a failure and didn't feel like anything was left for me except that mountain, the shop, those people, who I'd been told to be."

Graham continues to listen silently, giving me space to work this out and never letting up on the connection between our bodies.

"I hated myself—every inch of me—and I wanted to destroy myself for what I had done."

I can feel him flinch at this. It makes me cringe too. The harsh words I used to think about myself are so vicious; *I can't believe I was ever that cruel.*

"So, I did everything to try and punish myself, to forget you. I did things I'm not proud of..."

My confession is interrupted as Tommy rips around the corner on his horse. Graham lets me go. My first thought goes to Daniel and the panic in Graham's eyes lets me know his worries are there, too.

Tommy slows down and jumps off his horse. His eye is bloody and bruised. His lip is split; the beating looks fresh.

"Tommy, what happened?" Graham rushes over.

"I came as fast as I could. I barely got away in time. I didn't want to leave but Maggie made me go after you two."

We both wait as Tommy recovers and says, "It's Logan and the rest of them. His gang came down and took over."

Tommy looks directly at me. "He said things would be like they used to be if you don't go back and do your job. Ellie, he has your sisters."

A boulder drops back into my gut like I had not just lifted it and manually rolled it away myself. As if it had just been waiting to take its rightful place back. How selfish could I have been to leave? All of Aponi's words meant well but I just failed my sisters—again. No. *No. I'm not going there.*

Shaking my self-loathing off, I look at Graham. "Let's go."

We leave our tent and campsite. Tommy takes the cart while Graham and I take off toward town.

CHAPTER 30

Gunfire blasts off in the distance. My pulse quickens as we gallop into town. Harlots scatter throughout the town while drunken men and women crowd the main street. Fights break out and limp bodies litter the ground. Some are dead and some are passed out. Windows in the shops are broken. Scorched storefronts still smolder and Daniels's mercantile is dark and vacant. Placing a shaking hand on my holster, I scan the carnage. The sheriff is nowhere to be found, and I can't find my sisters or Daniel.

I spot Tricia on the corner, leaning her supple chest into the man in front of her. Tricia spots me too and runs into the saloon that is alive with music.

Graham and I dismount so we aren't sitting targets and raise our guns, ready for a fight.

From within the swinging doors, Logan appears with Maggie. Logan holds her naked arm, and the shoulder on her dress is ripped. Her cleavage is exposed in a way she would never choose to display herself. Logan's smile does not reach his eyes as he takes in my reaction with malice and satisfaction.

"Let her go, Logan." Graham's voice echoes through the street.

"You think you can order me around?" Logan sneers easily, shaking Maggie to make a point.

My whole body flexes.

"Just remember, I have your daddy, too. Don't think he will last much longer, though." Logan shrugs.

"Where have you taken him?" Grahams growls.

"I didn't come out here to talk to you, and if you say another word, Miss Maggie here will pay for it. You hear?" Logan raises his pistol to her head, pulls her in, and smells her mussed-up hair. He does this all while looking at me with intensity and unspoken threats. We both know what he's capable of.

"Ellie, you going to let that city boy fight your battles now?" Logan jerks his chin at Graham.

Graham takes a step forward. Snapping my eyes to Graham's, I raise my hand and push his gun down, shaking my head.

"That's right. Down, boy," Logan says, mocking Graham.

Graham's eyes are full of fire.

Trying to keep my voice steady, I say, "Logan, what do you want?" I don't lower my gun.

"I want you to come home. You belong up there with me." He motions around to the town. "Clearly, your absence has been missed."

"Logan, you made your point. Now let her go."

"Not until you come with me."

"Why are you doing this?"

"Because I'm sick of this town and these people acting like they have free rein on these parts. It needs to be known that they can't take what's ours." Logan's arm wraps around Maggie's chest and rests on the soft tissue spilling out of her bodice.

"Logan, get your hands off my sister."

"El, you jealous?" He bites his lip and cocks his head to the side, egging me on.

"Listen, you let her go, and you and I will talk about this, alone."

"You and I were never really good at talking. Now were we?" Logan looks at Graham and smiles cruelly.

Heat rises up my cheeks but my focus does not waver from getting my sister out of Logan's hands.

"Logan, that was a difficult time for me and you know it."

"That's right, and who was the only one that wanted you? Who stayed with you?" he challenges.

I can't bring myself to look at Graham.

"Ellie, don't listen to him." Maggie tries to shake Logan off. She rams her tiny elbow into his barrel chest. No reaction escapes him besides pulling her in closer.

"Ummmm, you have a little fight in you, too?" Logan kisses her exposed and elegant neck. Maggie stretches as far from him as she can.

Graham and I start to charge Logan but he cocks the hammer back. The gun is loaded and pressed with intention closer into my sister's temple. Logan's men and Tricia flank him and click behind him, echoing his readiness to fire, barrels pointing at our heads.

"Hey, honey, not so fast." Logan smiles again. "This is our town, our mountains. You are mine."

"Logan, I was never yours," I say as my anger overcomes me, "and that kills you."

"I think you are. I've had you more times. That makes you mine." Arrogance and malice coat his words.

I can't help the cringe that escapes my face. I look first at Maggie, her sad eyes meeting mine. Then I look at Graham in a silent apology.

"Shut your fucking mouth," Graham bellows.

Logan grabs Maggie's littlest finger, holds it up, and turns it in the wrong direction. The snap sounds like a thick branch, and her scream and cries follow.

"Not another word out of you, I said." Logan is icy and calm, challenging Graham by raising Maggie's next finger.

"Fuck you, Logan," I bellow, listening to Maggie's breathing that is quick, pained, and panicked.

"There's my girl. She's still in there. The swearing, fucking, and stealing outlaw I know she wants to be." Logan calls out all the things we did together in one smooth sentence.

"That was a dark time for me."

"I never forced you to do anything. You wanted it. Don't lie to yourself." Logan pokes at my holes.

My mind is trying to stay steady. But the unresolved guilt for all I did still simmers somewhere inside me. He tricked me into being a part of that man's death. *But he didn't force you to keep sleeping with him. He didn't force you to stay and ride along. You didn't stop any of it.* I continue to carry this guilt with me.

Logan knows how I was used to being talked to. He knows I talked to myself this way too. He used it before and he uses it now.

Logan takes advantage of my pause to stoke the flame of guilt and exposes all I had done to the people I love.

"That man's death is on your hands, too. Do you know what people are calling you? The Clancy Clan Queen. We didn't even have to get married and you took my name."

Everyone knows now. Fear and shame ooze down my spine; I can't keep my head up any longer. Turning to Graham, I see his eyes are wide, but I can't read what else he's thinking.

Logan continues, "That's right, El. No one will want you now that they know. We are your only way out. You are one of us and that will never change."

Lowering my gun, I feel the full brunt of what I've done laid out for all to know and hear. There's no hiding now.

"I will go with you," I say, "but you have to promise to let everyone go and that we'll leave town today."

Slowly, I put my gun on the ground and raise my hands before walking directly toward Logan, meeting his eyes with the playfulness and mirth I know will stir his desire. He smiles and rakes his gaze over my body.

"Let her go," I say just loudly enough so only Logan can hear me.

"A little closer, Ellie," Logan taunts.

Maggie's sweat and sadness at my surrender stare at me. "You deserve better than this. Don't give in."

Logan releases her and grabs for me as I murmur, "I am what I am. There is no changing the past."

I raise my voice for all to hear. "I'm messy and have done things I'm not proud of. The messy bits of me got me through my darkest hour, and if I hadn't gone there, I would have never saved myself. I do thank you for being there with me during that time of my life to push me to rock bottom. I needed to go there, and you shoved me into that pit. But I clawed my way back out, and neither you nor anyone else can make me feel bad about that. Because I have forgiven myself for all of that, and I don't need anyone else's approval except my own."

Logan's eyes narrow. "If I can't have you, then no one will."

Making sure Maggie is far enough away, I drop my arm so the knife in my sleeve falls into my hand. My grip is firm and sure. The knife in his hand drives into my side at the same time I drive my blade into the soft tissue of his neck.

Our eyes meet as his life slowly leaks out. Gunfire erupts around me as my body buckles under the weight of Logan falling forward. Graham's shots pick off Logan's backup one by one. Maggie takes out Tricia as she aims her fire at my head.

Maggie and Graham make quick work of the outlaws and rush over to me. I hold my side as blood gushes out.

Graham supports me on the ground as Maggie inspects the wound. My bloody hand releases my side as she pushes a handkerchief into the gash to stop the flow. Graham takes her place as she runs off.

Looking at Graham, I breathe, "I wanted to tell you, all of it, for myself. I'm so sorry."

"Don't you dare. How many times do I have to tell you? I love everything about you—including your messy bits."

Letting out a chuckle, I smile. "Good, because that's what you'll have with me—a big, bloody messy future."

Maggie returns with the doctor who assesses my wound. "Graham, pick her up and bring her to my office. It needs cleaning and sewing."

"Is she going to be all right?" Maggie asks urgently.

"Yes, it's just a flesh wound," reassures the doctor.

I'm relieved. My life, as myself, authentically and free, is going to exist.

CHAPTER 31

We know others might threaten our peace in the future. But for now, we have a stronghold throughout the towns, mountains, and valleys.

Maggie and Daniel rule the shop in town while Graham and I lead the routes and trades. Finding my voice gives me the energy to not only make friends along the way but also be known as the toughest businesswoman around. Graham insists I take over negotiations because of it.

Graham and I spend most of our time under the open sky between towns, happily tangled up with each other. We build a cabin to come home to after long trips away. The cabin is just outside of town on the way to the mountains and close to the river on a spot we claimed together.

Maggie and Daniel marry that year, and she's already showing signs of a swelling belly. Daniel always walks with a cane after his accident but this hasn't kept him from chasing Lottie and becoming her father. Their family is our family but also its own. It brings me so much joy to see them happy and complete.

Graham and I are to be married in the fall. The discussion of living separately has never been an issue since everyone already knows everything. No one seems to care except the old white-haired ladies who judge everyone anyway. It gives them something to do, Graham and I joke.

Part of my route, when we return to town, runs from the mercantile to the mountain. It's time for my first solo trip. Up until now, Tommy had taken over this task. He stayed up there more and more until eventually, he was brave enough to ask Maggie and me if he could take over the shop. Tommy said that he needed to make his own way, and I told him that the mountains and that cabin were the best places to sort it all out.

We both agreed he could have free rein over the place, so he moved in last month. Word had it he was doing well out there—not just at the shop, but also with Loretta the showgirl.

After our last long trip together, Graham needed to deal with inventory and annual planning. For some reason, this took him, Daniel, and Maggie to sort it all out. The discussion started last night over the dinner table and only stopped when they all were too tired to make any sense.

This morning, it has picked right back up in full swing over breakfast and coffee. Too many cooks are in that conversation, so I offer to take the supplies up to Tommy for the day. They all pause but then quickly agree and go back to their bickering. Watching them all together, hunched over in deep discussion, makes me smile.

Graham pauses just long enough to grab my face with two hands and deepen the kiss, leaving us both wanting more. Our lust flares, and we almost excuse ourselves to give in to our primal needs. But once Maggie suggests she take over more of the shop for her clothes, Graham reluctantly pulls away and returns to the table—but not before giving my backside a quick spank. Smoldering, Graham smiles at me as I roll my eyes and leave.

I'm sad to go but I haven't been back to the shop and cabin since I left all those months ago. It's time.

* * *

Gunpowder and I take our time. He knows the way, so I enjoy the scenery. I notice the sun hitting the rocks glistening from the runoff. The water running by trickles and gushes as the road meanders, winding up the path to my mountain. It feels like I'm able to appreciate the serenity of the present moment and not get distracted by my swirling thoughts to just gaze out over the vastness of this world and all that's in it. I think the word to describe this best is peace.

Making it the rest of the way to the cabin is a beautiful nostalgic climb back to where it all began.

I help Tommy and Loretta unload the supplies. They look happy. I can see the swell under Loretta's coat that she's trying to hide. Tommy gives me the money, and I'm soon on my way. I've already said goodbye to the cabin and am relieved that a new family will be in there to fill it with joy and life.

Gunpowder then points us toward Aponi's house. Smoke from the chimney fills the air just like I knew it always would. Rapping on the door makes Fin bark.

"Who could that be, Fin?" I hear Aponi ask her wolf.

Aponi opens the door and her face lights up at the sight of me. "My girl!"

We embrace tightly. She's like a safety blanket to me, and the warmth she gives me feels like home. Knowing she's still there continues to keep me steady.

Next, Fin and I nuzzle. He topples me over and licks my face. I pull some salmon jerky out for him, and he gobbles it right up.

Aponi steps back to inspect me. "I heard Logan paid your people a visit a while back. You held your own down there?"

"Only a little scratch." I lift my shirt to show her my scar.

"I'm sure glad to see you in one piece."

"I'm glad to be here."

Aponi ushers me in and makes us some tea. We catch up as if no time has passed. The ease of her presence relaxes me further.

She tells me all about her garden and how things have changed up here since Logan and his crew have left. The mountain and town have found peace at last.

Then, I tell her all about Maggie's clothing and how Graham and I spend most of our time on the road together.

Aponi sips the last of her tea and sets her mug down. Her expression shifts. She casts an intense gaze and levels her tone. "Ellie, I found something the other day while I was out hunting."

My guts tighten not knowing what she might have found that makes her this stoic.

"It was a pile of bones with this not too far away." Aponi pulls out the heavy black jacket that my daddy used to wear. She hands it to me. I can feel the weight of the flask in the jacket sloshing around as I try to balance it in my hands. No mistaking, this was his.

My hot tears flow.

"I didn't know when you would be back, so I dug a spot right next to your momma on the hillside." Aponi stands up and walks over to me, placing a hand on my shoulder. "I am sorry for your loss."

Nodding, I let the tears fall silently and without reservation. If I've learned one thing through all this it was to let the emotions out so they don't get a chance to fester inside. They ought to be released. I'm sad now but I am not sadness. Just like I am not anger when I am mad. My emotions are no longer enmeshed in who I am. I'm allowing them to be as I experience them, so I can let them go. This is the only way to shorten the uncomfortable ones.

Allowing my grief free rein, I accept her support once again and stay there as long as I need to.

It's about mid-day after I let myself process all this. I want to return to town before nightfall, but I have one last stop to make.

"Aponi, thank you for everything you've done for me."

She smiles. "It's goodbye for now. Just make sure you stop by whenever you can... or need to." Her eyes meet mine, and she lifts her gray eyebrows with a knowing angle. "You will be in trouble if you don't reach out when you need it. You hear?"

"I know." I hug her one last time longer and tighter than I ever do with most people. Then I slide into my daddy's oversized black coat.

Making my way to the bluff where both of my parents lay is not as gut-wrenching as I think it'll be. Seeing the two simple wooden crosses there is more comforting than sad. They are together—the way Daddy always wanted it to be.

"Well, Daddy, I did it. I survived this place. Maggie and Lottie are safe and taken care of. We are all fine. I want to thank you for teaching me how to survive. You gave me all the skills I needed to choose my own path, something that a lot of women don't get. You never understood how successful you were. You never needed to strike it rich. You already were. I hope you found peace as I have. Momma, thank you for teaching us softness and kindness. For encouraging us to follow love and our hearts. And, Momma, if you are with him, make sure he realizes how lucky he was to have a woman like you to walk this crazy life with."

Turning my face up to the sky, I see the clouds part, and rays from the sun warm my face. I absorb the heat that feels like a hug from them both.

Basking in the warm release of my attachment to all that was and all that might be, I feel truly free. To be me, to love, to forgive. Thankful for the good and the bad. For the relief and recovery that came from freeing myself and others from my desperate need to try and control an uncontrollable life.

Reaching down, I leave a bundle of blue and yellow delicate wildflowers on Momma's cross then take one last pull off Daddy's flask. I silently toast him before leaning it against his wooden resting place.

Pulling my daddy's jacket tighter, I take one last look at my parents together, sigh, and turn to go. Just as I turn to walk away, my vision catches on a pile of rocks that are out of place—just there to the left of Momma's plot. They are oddly positioned enough that I have to tilt my head. From this angle, they point in a V to the east. Following their weird point, I see in the distance, across the edge of the grassy knoll, a broken tree that snaps in the opposite direction.

I walk across the field, and my heart speeds up with my boots. My tracking skills propel me forward.

I reach the tree then quickly scan the ground and land in front of me. Nothing looks off or out of place here.

Rolling my eyes at myself and turning to head back forces my gaze skyward. There, midway up the tree, is another branch that did not naturally grow there—again, pointing east. Following its curious direction, I take off. Every so often, I look up and locate another branch high above my line of vision that is unnaturally resting in the canopy. No wind or natural order of things could have placed it there. Sweat starts to kiss my brow, and my heart hammers in my chest. The density of the trees opens up into a clearing.

There at the far end sits a thick pile of brush that looks like a thatch pile—burned and discarded. Edging closer, I realize it is covering something.

Ripping it away exposes a gaping hole deep in the ground. The trees serve as camouflage. Why would someone cover up this hole? Lowering myself into the hole, I light a match and hold it up. There just at eye level, glistening back at me, is a gold vein the size of my arm.

"Holy shit, Daddy. We did it."

THE END

ACKNOWLEDGMENTS

Thank you for reading my book. Ellie's journey is like many of ours in so many ways. Finding ourselves in a society and time where the pace is fast and the expectations are extremely high is the ultimate hero's journey. If you are brave enough to go there, your life can change drastically for the better. To live life on your own terms, by your own rules, and follow what you want out of life will surely set you free.

What really launched my journey to look inward was many years of chasing achievements and finding that they only gave me short-lived dopamine hits. Trust me when I say I'm still working on this. This book made me realize that even though publishing is a huge accomplishment, the experience gave me the most growth and joy.

To go after a dream that did not make any sense to my practical or logical brain but to my heart and soul was something I just had to do. This book is a form of living in authenticity and alignment for me. To write about worthiness as I continue to grapple with it was a deeply emotional and difficult task. It is the rawest, most real, and most meaningful venture I have ever embarked upon. As much as I hope Ellie's story helps others, this project was ultimately for me. Who knows what will come next, but I have learned trust in myself, deep confidence in who I am as a person, and how I want to live.

This is what "doing the damn thing" looks like. It broke me down and then built me back up over and over. It forced me to be imperfect while making decisions and moving forward so as not to get stuck in the overwhelm. I had to reach out for support over and over again throughout the whole process, in many ways, and from many people. This forced me to get over asking for help. That presale campaign was *huge* for an independent people pleaser who hates asking for anything.

Most of all, I want you to know that you do not have to do it alone. Many forms of wise mentors support me through this messy, beautiful, difficult, and wonderful life. When I say I didn't do it alone, I mean it.

To my husband Steven; you are a wild, adventurous, and wickedly smart human. Your zest for life and living it to the fullest inspires me every day. You pushed me to just start—no need for the fanciest tools or the perfect situation. You encouraged me to try, learn, try again, and then learn some more. This built so much confidence in myself. I know this book took a lot of time, but I appreciate your love throughout it. I couldn't have done this at this time, with all this freedom, in the way I wanted to do it, without you.

Meggan, my big sister, you were the first to hear the early story of my wild mountain woman. I still remember the look on your face; your excitement and your response were what I needed to start believing in myself. You made me think I might actually have a really great story. Everyone needs a Meggan in their corner, and I'm thankful every day you're in mine.

To Mom, Dad, and little sister Erika, thank you for listening. Your interest, check-ins, and encouragement to continue were so appreciated and honestly needed at times. The hours you spent listening to my struggles and triumphs while helping me process it all is something every author needs, and I thank you for supporting this crazy idea.

My best friend Sasha, you reminded me that I wanted to be a writer. When I told you I was going to write a book, your unsurprised expression made me laugh out loud. You remembered that high school version of me, the one I had totally forgotten, and your unfazed response solidified for me that I am on the right path. You know me better, if not the best, and your steadfast belief in me and your commitment to our continued growth are so cherished.

Duane Green PhD., you were the first to help me see myself more clearly and to advocate for myself. You helped me in my deepest, most difficult hours of need, and I would not want anyone else to have been there for me through the darkest night of my soul. Aponi's ability to see right through Ellie's shields is what you were for me. Mental health is deeply underutilized, complex, and difficult. I thank God you pursued it and I found you.

Kristen Walker. Oh, where do I start? You helped me hope and dream again. You validated *all* of my feelings. Your persistent clarity and wisdom were the sunlight beam I needed to follow until I could understand and actually believe I have my own light to radiate. You, my dear friend, are a gift to this world. If you actually want to transform your life, go to clarityonfire.com. Consume their podcasts and get coached.

To Carol Wright, you came into my life during this process and have been here to remind me of the importance of it, prioritizing myself and my needs during this transformative experience. You are Aponi in so many ways. I began to write her before I ever knew you but then really understood her once you became part of my life. I think this is the ultimate form of a higher power and manifestation, and I thank God that we met. Thank you for reminding me to play and to let the little girl in the tutu and leather jacket twirl around and burn things when she needs to.

My dear friend Gin Howerton, you are my ultimate cheerleader and soul sister. I still believe we were related in a different life. I feel like we are just getting started. You are so loved and cherished. When I doubted myself the most, I pictured I was writing it just for you. That helped me be kinder to myself and less scared to write from the heart. Pretending that only you were going to read it helped me more than you know. Your compassion and light are so needed. If you want a born, natural, energy healer, she is your lady and can be found at ropanahealing.com.

Professor Eric Koester, you are a force of nature and are simply awe-inspiring. That call last September 30, 2021, which happened to be on my birthday, shot a lightning bolt into my life. It was the best birthday present I could have received. Your steadfast belief in me, the support you have created, the community, and innovation are difficult to put into words because you illicit feeling and passion. There is no way to show or tell people about it unless they experience your energy firsthand. Thank you for creating the Creator Institute and giving authors a way to make their dreams come true. If you are thinking about writing a book, I cannot recommend his program more. In the words of the great Eric Koester, "Never write alone."

Professor Hayley Newlin, you were the first to say, "Yes, you are an author. Now proclaim it." Your belief in me and my writing gave me the staying confidence to continue. To be a horror writer, with dark preferences and a dynamic presence, yet also be the sweetest and most supportive professor is a strong example for your students, especially women, that you can be anything you want.

Nicole Spindler and Hayley are a one-two punch. Your calmness and steadfast support in this program were the reassuring pat on the back I needed. Thank you.

To my editor Whitney McGruder, you were on board with my vision from the beginning. Your belief in my story drove it home for me. Thank you for handling my baby and me with such gentleness. Thank you for being there through the most grueling part of this process. You are the warrior princess I would want next to me on any journey. You are another example of a feminine powerhouse, and I look up to you in so many ways.

Nana, you ignited my interest in storytelling from a young age. You are the wisest and most beloved wise woman in my life. To Papa for having the vision and allowing me to grow up in such a beautiful place.

To my recently deceased grandma, Virginia White, your value in books and language elevated my expectations and drive to not only tell a story but become a skilled writer. Thank you for all the hours you spent editing my work. I truly believe it was in preparation for this book.

And finally, thank you to my presale supporters. I was overwhelmed by all the love I received from all corners of my life. I could not have done this without you:

Jeff Stone, Lisa Hart, Dale White, Jamie Pollock, Paulina Staab, Rachelle Brisbois, Desiree Torres, Kerry Finn, Cassie Mueller, Juliana Laury, Audra & Matty Straughn, Hillary Bageant, Cooky La Madrid, Carol Hough, Emilee Arner, Uncle Tim White, Leslie Wiese, Aunt Meg Lennox, Jerri Duncan, Janet Kobylarz, Scott Strongin, Lisa Schultz & Nate Gardner , Brenda Brown, Gin & Nate Howerton, Deb Storms, Becca Persen, Haley Mills, Eric Koester, Aunt Jody Schneidmiller, Ellen Carlos, Shannon Green & Mike Metzger, Mother and

Father in Law Diane & Tom Metzger, Jamie Hillman, Becky Lee, Jennifer Keon, Kelsi Hargrove, Cori Jones, Connie Langford, Allison Prell, Mark Guzman, Holly Lundberg, Kristen Walker, Shannon Stelzer, Sebastian Lopez, Michelle Trower, Jennifer Harris, Leigh Bowe, Melanie Heimark, Molly Loncosty, Kate Reed, Jennifer Boone, Danielle Erke, Tamara Mayo, Cookie & Mike Green, Ashley Bruns, Dayton Allemand, Annie Frederick, Boomer Mobley, Sam Lacanlale, Roberta Chang, Vishanka Gandhi, Jerrie Heyamoto, Leslie Whigham, Dani Fergen, Brittney Robinson, Stacy Peterson, Jamie Welch, Kelsee Ellison, Michelle Fazio, Katy Anderson, Holly Mehrer, Amber Swain, Richele & Zac Taylor, Sarah Grisier, Andrea Ward, Shellabi Koffi, Francisca Hernandez, Eileen Sheehan, Rebecca Garner, Jeanne Godfroy, Allison Johnson, Lisa Bowman, Martha Winje, Holly Schneidmiller, Liberty Hoffer, Mom Wilma & Dad Kevin Hahn, Jessica Washington, Laura MacLeod, Susan Willenbrock, Amber Jolley, Lois Robertson, Rori Matthai, Shelly Goldstein, Scott Nordahl, Noah Wagar, Dinalynn Rosenbush, Sasha Buckley, Sue Mauro, Susanne Reichart, Allen Roedel, Annie Naccarato, Craig Robertson, Annie Henson, Gabe Almack, Megan Cox, Teagan Sigler, Chris & Gail Morris, BreAnne Crow, Pam Sherman, Jamie LaRoque, Brooke Jurgens, Tori Thurman, Brett & Autumn Eckenrod, Christy Carter, Aunt Laura Smith, Kindra Miiller, Riley Fisher, James Brown, Big Sister Meggan Pape, Donna Le Valley, Jennifer Henjum, Meghan Young, Mariya Vasyu, Cindi Warburton, Monica Dagusen, Jake Deakins, Ashley Findlay, Janet Decker, Samantha Gardner, Sonia Wink, Torey Healea, Victoria Reece, Laura White, Josh Beers, Katie Sonnemaker-Denton, Colleen Smith, Michael Woodruff, Brandi Essman, Abigail Ward, Jina Haley, Alyx Kay, Husband Steven Metzger, Debbie Buckley, Lainey Seversike, Josh Bolton, Samual Bush, Jasmine Gayle, Sara Babcock, Ellen

Archibeque, Little Sister Erika Hahn, Philip Lenoue III, Jillian Cowden, Aimee Gence, Shona Koehn, Kyle Sullivan, Anne Mayer, Jason & Brittany Totland, Shannon Pelley, Samantha Schneider, JoAnne Farmin, Amy Anderson, Brenda Yahne, Heidi Greenfield, Hilary Schneidmiller, Marianne Nichols, Kelsey Phillips, Doris McCroskey, Mitch and Megan Tippetts, Nana and Papa Hahn, Lennart Hellberg, Nancy & Larry Sauer.

Made in the USA
Columbia, SC
15 October 2022